United States Government Accountability Office

GAO

Report to the Chairman, Special
Committee on Aging, U.S. Senate

I0415845

July 2012

RETIREMENT SECURITY

Women Still Face Challenges

GAO
Accountability ★ Integrity ★ Reliability

July 2012

RETIREMENT SECURITY
Women Still Face Challenges

Why GAO Did This Study

Elderly women, who comprise a growing portion of the U.S. population, have historically been at greater risk of living in poverty than elderly men. Several factors contribute to the higher rate of poverty among elderly women including their tendency to have lower lifetime earnings, take time out of the workforce to care for family members, and outlive their spouses. Other factors could affect older women's financial insecurity. These include the economic downturn and changing trends in pension plan offerings. In light of these circumstances, GAO was asked to examine (1) how women's access to and participation in employer-sponsored retirement plans compare to men's and how they have changed over time, (2) how women's retirement income compares to men's and how the composition of their income—the proportion of income coming from different sources—changed with economic conditions and trends in pension design, (3) how later-in-life events affect women's retirement income security, and (4) what policy options are available to help increase women's retirement income security. To answer these questions, GAO analyzed data from two nationally representative surveys, conducted a broad literature review, and interviewed a range of experts in the area of retirement security.

GAO is making no recommendations. GAO received technical comments on a draft of this report from the Department of Labor, the Department of the Treasury and the Social Security Administration, and incorporated them, as appropriate.

View GAO-12-699. For more information, contact Charles Jeszeck at (202) 512-7215 or jeszeckc@gao.gov.

What GAO Found

Over the last decade, working women's access to and participation in employer-sponsored retirement plans have improved relative to men. Indeed, from 1998 to 2009, women surpassed men in their likelihood of working for an employer that offered a pension plan, largely because the proportion of men covered by a plan declined. Furthermore, as employers have continued to terminate their defined benefit (DB) plans and have switched to defined contribution (DC) plans, the proportion of women who worked for employers that offered a DC plan increased. Correspondingly, women's participation rates in DC plans increased slightly over this same period while men's participation fell, thereby narrowing the participation difference between men and women to 1 percentage point. At the same time, however, women contributed to their DC plans at lower levels than men.

Although the composition of income for women age 65 and over did not vary greatly over the period—despite changes in the economy and pension system—women continued to have less retirement income on average and live in higher rates of poverty than men in that age group. The composition of women's income varied only slightly, in part, because their main income sources—Social Security and DB benefits—were shielded from fluctuations in the market. Women, especially widows and those age 80 and over, depended on Social Security benefits for a larger percentage of their income than men. For example, in 2010, 16 percent of women age 65 and over depended solely on Social Security for income compared to 12 percent of men. At the same time, the share of household income women received from earnings increased over the period, but was consistently lower than for men. Moreover, women's median income was approximately 25 percent lower than men's over the last decade, and the poverty rate for women in this age group was nearly two times higher than men's in 2010.

For women approaching or in retirement, becoming divorced, widowed or unemployed had detrimental effects on their income security. Moreover, divorce and widowhood had more pronounced effects for women than for men. For example, women's household income, on average, fell by 41 percent with divorce, almost twice the size of the decline that men experienced. For widowhood, women's household income fell by 37 percent—while men's declined by only 22 percent. Unemployment also had a detrimental effect on income security, though the effects were similar for women and men; household assets and income fell by 7 to 9 percent.

A range of existing policy options could address some of the income security challenges women face in retirement. For example, some would expand existing tax incentives to save for retirement while others would improve access to annuities. All of these options have advantages and disadvantages that would need to be evaluated prior to implementation. For example, increasing Social Security benefits for widows could provide additional income for women who have few options to increase their retirement savings. However, increasing benefits would also increase costs to the Social Security program and have implications for its long-term solvency.

Contents

Letter		1
	Background	4
	Working Women's Access to and Participation in Employer-Sponsored Pension Plans Have Improved Relative to Men	9
	While Income Composition Changed Only Slightly for Women Age 65 and Over, They Continue to Have Less Retirement Income Than Men	18
	Divorce, Widowhood, and Unemployment Had a Detrimental Effect on Older Women's Income Security	27
	Existing Policy Options Could Address Retirement Security Issues Facing Women	36
	Concluding Observations	46
	Agency Comments	47

Appendix I	Objective, Scope, and Methods	49
	Section 1: Information Sources	49
	Section 2: Methods for Comparing Working Women's and Men's Access to and Participation in Employer-Sponsored Pension Plans	54
	Section 3: Methods for Comparing the Income of Women and Men Age 65 and Over	73
	Section 4: Methods for Analyzing the Effects of Events Occurring Later in Life on Women's and Men's Household Income and Assets	74

Appendix II	GAO Contact and Staff Acknowledgments	89

Tables		
	Table 1: Estimated Effects of Life Events on Household Assets and Income by Gender	28
	Table 2: Percent of Women and Men Reporting Their Health Is Poor Is Similar across Age Groups	35
	Table 3: Proposals to Expand Use of Existing Tax Incentives to Save for Retirement	37
	Table 4: Proposals to Expand Eligibility and Opportunities to Accumulate Social Security Credits	39
	Table 5: Proposals to Expand Access to Retirement Savings and Strengthen Spousal Protections	40

Table 6: Proposals to Expand Opportunities for Saving Later in Life and Delay Social Security Benefit Receipt | 41
Table 7: Proposals to Ensure Lifetime Income | 43
Table 8: Proposals to Ensure Income Adequacy | 44
Table 9: Data Sources Used for Each Reporting Objective | 49
Table 10: SIPP Panels, Waves, and Questionnaires Used to Answer Objective 1 and Objective 2 | 50
Table 11: Birth Years for the HRS Cohorts and the Year Data Collection Began for Each Cohort | 52
Table 12: Information Used from SIPP to Construct Key Variables | 55
Table 13: Characteristics of the Working Population over Time | 58
Table 14: Factors Associated with Working for an Employer That Offers a Plan, 2009 | 63
Table 15: Factors Associated with Eligibility for Employer-Sponsored Pension Plan, 2009 | 67
Table 16: Factors Associated with Participation in an Employer-Sponsored Pension Plan, 2009 | 70
Table 17: Descriptive Statistics of Women and Men in the HRS by Age | 76
Table 18: Proportion of Individuals Changing Status between Observations | 79
Table 19: Divorce Effect on Household Assets and Income | 84
Table 20: Widowhood Effect on Household Assets and Income | 85
Table 21: Unemployment Effect | 86
Table 22: A Decline in Health's Effect on Household Assets and Income | 87
Table 23: Effects of Providing Financial Assistance or Physical Care on Household Assets and Income | 88

Figures

Figure 1: Labor Force Participation Rates for Women, Ages 25 to 64 | 5
Figure 2: In 2009, Working Women and Working Men Were Similar in Their Access to and Participation in Employer-Sponsored Pension Plans | 10
Figure 3: Proportion of Working Women and Men with Employers That Offered Any Type of Pension Plan and DC Plans Specifically | 11
Figure 4: The Proportion of Working Women and Working Men with Employers That Offered DC Pension Plans Varied, by Race | 13

Figure 5: The Proportion of Working Women and Men Who Were Eligible for Their Employer's Pension Plans (among the Population Whose Employers Offered a Plan)   14

Figure 6: The Proportion of Eligible Women and Men That Participated in Any Type of Employer-Sponsored Pension Plan or in DC Plans (among the Population That Was Eligible for a Plan)   15

Figure 7: The Proportion of Working Women and Working Men (among Those Who Were Eligible) Who Participated in Their Employer's Defined Contribution Pension Plans, by Race   16

Figure 8: The Composition of Household Income for Women and Men Age 65 and Over Did Not Fluctuate Greatly Over Time   19

Figure 9: Differences in the Composition of Household Income for Women and Men Age 65 and Over, by Marital Status, 2010   20

Figure 10: Differences in the Composition of Household Income for Women and Men Age 65 and Over, by Age Group, 2010   21

Figure 11: Differences in the Composition of Household Income for Women and Men Age 65 and Over, by Race and Ethnicity, 2010   23

Figure 12: Median Household Incomes in 2010 for Individuals 65 and Over by Age Group   25

Figure 13: Poverty Rates by Demographic Categories in 2010 for Women and Men Age 65 and Over   26

Figure 14: Estimated Effects of Divorce and Separation on Total Household Assets and Income   30

Figure 15: Estimated Effects of Widowhood on Total Household Assets and Income   32

Figure 16: Estimated Effects of Unemployment on Total Household Assets and Income   33

Figure 17: Estimated Effects of a Decline in Health on Total Household Assets and Income   34

Abbreviations

AHEAD	Asset and Health Dynamics of the Oldest Old
CODA	Children of the Depression Era
DB	defined benefit
DC	defined contribution
ERISA	Employee Retirement Income Security Act of 1974
HRS	Health and Retirement Study
IRA	individual retirement account
SCF	Survey of Consumer Finances
SIPP	Survey of Income and Program Participation

United States Government Accountability Office
Washington, DC 20548

July 19, 2012

The Honorable Herb Kohl
Chairman
Special Committee on Aging
United States Senate

Dear Mr. Chairman,

Historically, elderly women have been at greater risk of living in poverty than elderly men. Several economic and demographic factors contribute to their higher poverty rates in old age. First, women's average annual earnings are consistently lower than men's. Second, women are more likely to take time out of the workforce to care for children and elderly relatives. These employment patterns result in lower retirement savings, reduced Social Security benefits,[1] and smaller pension benefits for women in comparison to men. Third, women tend to live longer than men, increasing the risk of exhausting their retirement savings before death. Finally, women are more likely than men to live alone in old age,[2] increasing their vulnerability to unexpected economic and health shocks due to the inability to pool resources with a partner or benefit from spousal care-giving in the event of an illness.

Recent economic events affecting both men and women have the potential to exacerbate older women's financial insecurity. The financial crisis and recent recession have resulted in depressed home values and high unemployment rates among younger and older Americans alike. At the same time, health care costs continue to rise. Efforts to address the financial challenges of Social Security and Medicare could lead to a

---

[1]Generally, Social Security retirement benefits are based on up to 35 years of a worker's indexed earnings. Average lower earnings over a lifetime and fewer years in the workforce lead to significantly lower average benefit amounts for women as compared to men. In 2009, the average annual Social Security income received by retired women was $12,155 compared to $15,620 for men, according to one study. See Carroll L. Estes, Terry O'Neill and Heidi Hartmann, *Breaking the Social Security Glass Ceiling: A Proposal to Modernize Women's Benefits*, Institute for Women's Policy Research, National Committee to Preserve Social Security & Medicare Foundation, and National Organization for Women Foundation (May 2012).

[2]This is due to at least two factors: women have longer life expectancies, and in marriages the husband is, on average, older than the wife by 3 years.

GAO-12-699 Women's Retirement Security

reduction in benefits for retirees.[3] In addition, the burden of saving for retirement and paying for old-age health care has been shifting from employers to employees in both the private and public sectors. In the private sector, for example, many employers continue to replace defined benefit (DB) pension plans with defined contribution (DC) plans and reduce or eliminate retiree health insurance benefits. At the same time, many employed in the public sector have seen a reduction in their pension benefits or an increase in employee contributions for those benefits.

In light of this unique confluence of circumstances, the Senate Special Committee on Aging requested that we explore the issue of women's retirement income security with a special focus on the effects of the recent financial crisis and subsequent recession, and the persistent trend of employers to replace DB with DC plans.[4] Specifically, this report examines (1) how women's access to and participation in employer-sponsored retirement plans compare to men's and how they have changed over time, (2) how women's retirement income compares to men's and how the composition of their income changed with economic conditions and trends in pension design, (3) how events occurring later in life affect women's retirement income security, and (4) what policy options are available to help increase women's retirement income security.

To address these questions, we analyzed two nationally-representative datasets, conducted an extensive literature review, and consulted with numerous experts. Specifically, to analyze plan coverage and participation rates among the working-age population, we used data for the late 1990s through 2009 from the Survey of Income and Program Participation (SIPP), a nationally-representative survey.[5] With these data,

---

[3]In 2008, about 69 percent of single women 65 and over living alone would have been living in poverty if it were not for Social Security benefits they received, according to a study published by the Institute for Women's Policy Research. See Jeff Hayes, Heidi Hartmann, and Sunhwa Lee, *Social Security: Vital to Retirement Security for 35 Million Women and Men,* Institute for Women's Policy Research Briefing Paper, IWPR Publication #D487 (March 2010).

[4]This report builds upon our past work for this committee. See GAO, *Retirement Security: Women Face Challenges in Ensuring Financial Security in Retirement,* GAO-08-105 (Washington, D.C.: Oct. 11, 2007).

[5]Specifically, we used data from the 1996, 2001, 2004, and 2008 SIPP panel surveys, which are administered over a period of several years.

we computed descriptive statistics on plan coverage, eligibility, and participation rates and conducted an econometric analysis of each of these. To analyze median incomes and the income composition of the retirement-age population, we computed descriptive statistics using SIPP data from the late 1990s through 2010.[6] To understand the factors that affect women's income and assets, we developed a statistical model to estimate the effects of events occurring later in life, such as widowhood, using the Health and Retirement Study (HRS), a nationally representative dataset that tracks Americans 51 years or older over time.[7] We conducted a data reliability assessment of selected SIPP and HRS data and found that, for the purposes of our analysis, the data that we analyzed were sufficiently reliable. Finally, to identify policy options that could increase retirement income security among women, we conducted an extensive literature review and interviewed a range of experts in the area of retirement income security.[8]

We conducted this performance audit from March 2011 through July 2012 in accordance with generally accepted government auditing standards. Those standards require that we plan and perform the audit to obtain sufficient, appropriate evidence to provide a reasonable basis for our findings and conclusions based on our audit objectives. We believe that the evidence we obtained provides a reasonable basis for our findings and conclusions based on our audit objectives. For more information on our scope and methodology, see appendix I.

---

[6]Data on income were available through 2010, while data on retirement plan coverage and participation were only available through 2009.

[7]Specifically, we used a statistical technique called "fixed-effects regression." Because the HRS tracks individuals over time, we were able to estimate the percentage change in household income and assets that occurs for an individual after a life event, relative to an individual that did not experience that life event, but also became older. In this way, we were able to isolate the effect of the life event from other factors. We used all available years of HRS data, including early release data for 2010. For more information on methods, see appendix I.

[8]To ensure that we obtained a balanced perspective, we interviewed experts with a range of viewpoints and from different types of organizations including government, academia, advocacy groups, and the private sector. For a list of organizations, see appendix I.

Background

Demographic and Labor Force Trends Affecting Women's Retirement Income Security

Since the early 1900s, female life expectancy has exceeded male life expectancy, resulting in women outnumbering men in the older age groups. Although gender differences in life expectancy have been decreasing, women age 65 and over continue to outnumber men age 65 and over. This trend is projected to continue over the next 4 decades. Further, the population age 65 and over is expected to more than double from 2010 to 2050.[9] The population of women among the "oldest-old"—those 85 and over—is also projected to grow.[10] Today, of those age 65 and over, one-sixth of women and one-tenth of men are among the oldest-old and this is projected to grow to almost one-quarter of women and one-fifth of all men by 2050.[11]

Women's workforce participation surged over the last half of the 20th century. Among women ages 25 to 54, the rate of labor force participation jumped from 42 percent by the end of the 1950s to about 74 percent by the late 1980s. The rate continued to grow in the 1990s but at a slower pace. Over the last decade, the rate declined slightly from its peak of 76.8 percent in 1999, and was 74.7 percent in 2011. Labor force participation rates have varied by generation, with women born in the baby boom generation much more likely to be in the workforce than preceding generations.[12] As baby boomers have aged, workforce participation rates have increased significantly for women ages 55 to 64 (see fig. 1).

---

[9]Linda A. Jacobsen, Mary Kent, Marlene Lee, and Mark Mather, "America's Aging Population," *Population Bulletin*, Population Reference Bureau, vol. 66, no. 1 (2011).

[10]*Ibid.*

[11]*Ibid.*

[12]The baby boom generation consists of individuals born from 1946 to 1964.

Figure 1: Labor Force Participation Rates for Women, Ages 25 to 64

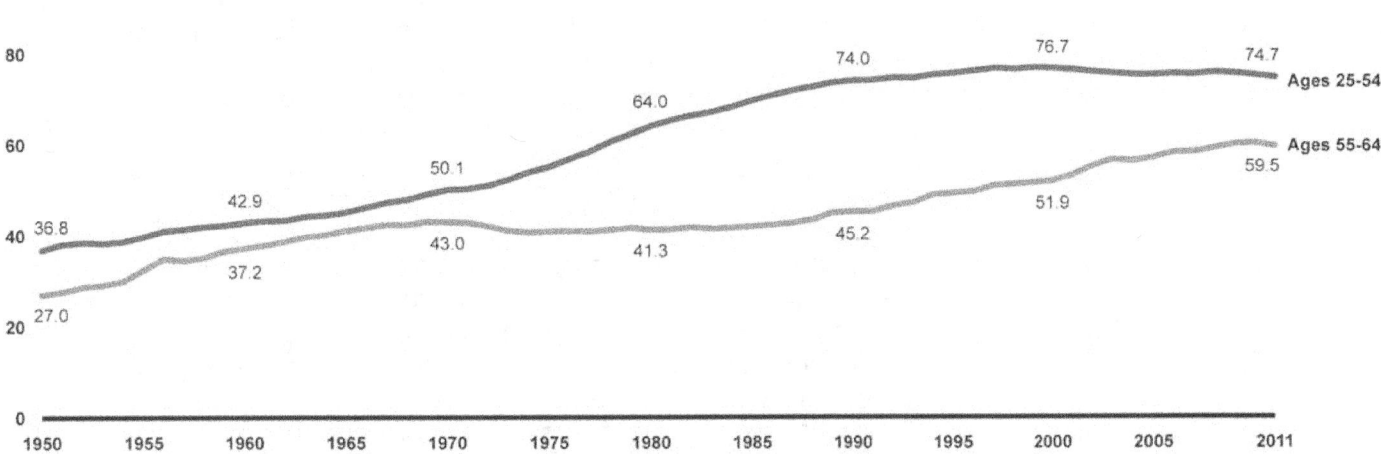

Source: GAO analysis of BLS data.

Despite their economic gains, women continue to have lower annual earnings than men, on average, and much lower lifetime earnings. In 2010, the median earnings of women working full-time were about $36,900, compared to $47,700 for men.[13] One study reported that a 25-year-old woman with a college degree will make about $523,000 less in wages over her lifetime compared to a man with a college degree.[14] Further, the study noted that of those retiring at age 62 in 2000, women were in the workforce for 12 years less than men, on average, primarily because they spent more time than men out of the workforce caring for family members.[15]

---

[13]Carmen DeNavas-Walt, Bernadette D. Proctor, and Jessica C. Smith, "Income, Poverty, and Health Insurance Coverage in the United States: 2010" *Current Population Reports, Consumer Income,* United States Census Bureau, P60-239 (September 2011).

[14]Cindy Hounsell, *The Female Factor 2008: Why Women Are at Greater Financial Risk in Retirement and How Annuities Can Help* (Washington, D.C.: Americans for Secure Retirement, 2008).

[15]*Ibid.*

GAO-12-699 Women's Retirement Security

Sources of Retirement Income

Although the composition of retirement income—the proportion of income coming from different sources—varies greatly for individual households, Social Security benefits, pension income, and earnings make up the bulk of income for the U.S. population age 65 and over. Social Security provides retirement benefits to eligible workers, based on their work and earnings history. Social Security also provides benefits to eligible workers who become disabled before reaching retirement age, as well as spouses, widow(er)s, and children of eligible workers. Although all Social Security benefits are based upon a common formula, they are calculated in different ways for each beneficiary type.[16] The level of the monthly benefit is adjusted for inflation and varies depending on the age at which the beneficiary chooses to begin receiving benefits. Generally, beneficiaries may begin receiving retirement benefits at age 62; however, the payments will be higher if they wait to receive benefits at their full retirement age, which varies from 65 to 67, depending on the beneficiary's birth year. The monthly retirement benefit continues to rise for workers who delay benefits beyond their full retirement age, up to age 70. Employees and employers pay payroll taxes that finance Social Security benefits. However, Social Security faces a long-term financing shortfall resulting largely from lower birth rates and longer life spans. According to the Social Security Trustees, the Social Security Trust Funds could be exhausted by 2033 and unable to pay full benefits.[17]

Pension income from employer-provided retirement plans falls into two broad categories: DB and DC pension plans. DB plans typically provide retirement benefits to each retiree in the form of an annuity that provides a monthly payment for life, the value of which is typically determined by a formula based on particular factors specified by the plan, such as salary or years of service. Under DC plans, workers and employers may make

---

[16]For example, wives may be eligible to receive a spousal benefit equal to 50 percent of their husbands' benefits. If a wife receiving this benefit becomes widowed, then the benefit becomes a survivor benefit, and may equal up to 100 percent of the husband's benefit. For more information on how the different types of benefits are calculated, see GAO, *Social Security Reform: Issues for Disability and Dependent Benefits*, GAO-08-26 (Washington, D.C.: Oct. 26, 2007).

[17]The Board of Trustees, Federal Old-Age and Survivors Insurance and Federal Disability Insurance Trust Funds, *The 2012 Annual Report of the Board of Trustees of the Federal Old-Age and Survivors Insurance and Federal Disability Insurance Trust Funds* (Washington, D.C.: Apr. 25, 2012).

contributions into individual accounts.[18] Workers can also save for retirement through an individual retirement account (IRA). IRAs allow workers to receive favorable tax treatment for making contributions to an individual account.[19]

At retirement, participants' distribution options vary depending on the type of pension plan. Private sector DB plans must offer participants a benefit in the form of a lifetime annuity (either immediately or deferred). An annuity can help to protect a retiree against risks, including the risk of outliving one's assets (longevity risk) and, when an inflation-adjusted annuity is provided, the risk of inflation diminishing one's purchasing power. Some DB plans also give participants a choice to take a lump sum cash settlement (distribution) or roll over funds to an IRA, instead of taking a lifetime annuity.[20] In contrast, DC plan sponsors are not required to offer a lifetime annuity and more often provide participants with a lump sum distribution as the only option. Other options for DC participants may include leaving money in the plan, taking a partial distribution, rolling their plan savings into an IRA, or purchasing an annuity, which are typically only available outside of the plan.

In addition, whether a pension plan is a DB or DC has implications for whether a spouse is entitled to the pension's benefits. The Employee Retirement Income Security Act of 1974 (ERISA) requires that DB plans include a survivor's benefit, called a qualified joint and survivor annuity. Thus, after a worker with a DB plan dies, the surviving spouse continues to receive an annuity, but typically at a reduced level.[21] A qualified joint and survivor annuity may only be waived through a written spousal consent. Under most DC plans, the plan is written so that the employee

---

[18]The most common type of DC plans are 401(k) plans, which typically allow workers to choose to contribute a portion of their pretax compensation to the plan.

[19]The tax treatment differs depending on the type of IRA. For example, with traditional IRAs, workers who meet certain conditions can take an income tax deduction on some or all of the contributions they make to their IRA, but they must pay taxes on amounts they withdraw from the IRA. Workers below certain income limits may also contribute to Roth IRAs, which do not provide an income tax deduction on contributions, but permit tax-free withdrawals after a specified time period.

[20]Rolling funds over to an IRA allows participants to preserve the tax benefits enjoyed by the plan.

[21]The qualified joint and survivor annuity must provide at least a 50 percent benefit continuation to the surviving spouse.

may, during his or her lifetime, make withdrawals from the account or roll over the balance into an IRA without spousal consent, provided that the employee's vested account balance is payable in full on death to the surviving spouse.

National Trends Affecting Retirement Security for Men and Women

Over the past quarter-century, the percentage of private sector workers participating in employer-sponsored pension plans has held steady at about 50 percent. Although some workers choose not to participate in an employer-sponsored pension plan, the large majority of nonparticipating workers do not have access to one.[22] In addition, over the last 3 decades, the U.S. retirement system has undergone a major transition from one based primarily on DB plans to one based on DC plans, increasing workers' exposure to economic volatility and usually shifting the burden of saving to the individual worker, which makes them more reliant on their own decision making. As we have previously reported, from 1990 to 2008, the number of active participants in private sector DB plans fell by 28 percent, from about 26 million to about 19 million. Over the same period, the number of active participants in DC plans increased by 90 percent, from about 35 million to about 67 million.[23] DC plans generally do not offer annuities, so retirees are left with increasingly important decisions about managing their retirement savings to ensure they have income throughout retirement.[24] These decisions may be more difficult to make in times of economic volatility. For example, two recent recessions—one beginning in March 2001 and ending in November 2001 and the other beginning in December 2007 and ending in June 2009[25]— resulted in major stock indices falling dramatically. The long-term effects of financial market fluctuations on retirement income security are

---

[22]GAO, *Retirement Savings: Automatic Enrollment Shows Promise for Some Workers, but Proposals to Broaden Retirement Savings for Other Workers Could Face Challenges*, GAO-10-31 (Washington, D.C.: Oct. 23, 2009).

[23]GAO, *Retirement Income: Ensuring Income throughout Retirement Requires Difficult Choices*, GAO-11-400 (Washington, D.C.: June 7, 2011).

[24]DC participants can purchase annuities on the retail market. However, retail annuities are typically more expensive for women than for men because of women's longer life expectancy, whereas in-plan annuity options, when they are offered, must be at gender-neutral rates. In addition, in-plan rates may be lower than retail rates because the in-plan rate may be able to take advantage of a lower, institutional price. Nonetheless, research shows that most people choose not to annuitize DC savings.

[25]These recession periods were identified by the National Bureau of Economic Research Business Cycle Dating Committee.

uncertain, but the effects may vary based on factors such as age, type of pension plan, and employment status.[26] Employment status, in particular, can pose serious challenges for retirement security. As we recently reported, long-term unemployment can reduce an older worker's future monthly retirement income in numerous ways such as by reducing the number of years the worker can accumulate DB plan retirement benefits or DC plan savings, by motivating workers to claim Social Security at an earlier age, and by leading workers to draw down retirement savings to pay for expenses during unemployment.[27]

Working Women's Access to and Participation in Employer-Sponsored Pension Plans Have Improved Relative to Men

From 1998 to 2009, working women surpassed men in their likelihood of having an employer that offered a pension plan, but were slightly less likely to be eligible for and to participate in those plans.[28] However, this gap, narrowed over time. In fact, by 2009, the same proportion of working women and men ultimately participated in some type of plan (either a DB or a DC) as shown in figure 2. Nonetheless, women's contribution rates to DC plans remained lower than those of men.

---

[26]GAO, *Private Pensions: Some Key Features Lead to an Uneven Distribution of Benefits*, GAO-11-333 (Washington, D.C.: Mar. 30, 2011).

[27]See GAO, *Unemployed Older Workers: Many Experience Challenges Regaining Employment and Face Reduced Retirement Security*, GAO-12-445 (Washington, D.C.: Apr. 25, 2012).

[28]The statistics we present in this section are unadjusted point estimates computed from the SIPP data without taking into account differences between men and women in demographic and occupational characteristics. To adjust these point estimates by taking into account different factors that might explain gender differences in these three outcomes—working for an employer that offers a plan, plan eligibility, and participation—we also conducted multivariate analysis. The detailed results of these analyses are presented in appendix I.

Figure 2: In 2009, Working Women and Working Men Were Similar in Their Access to and Participation in Employer-Sponsored Pension Plans

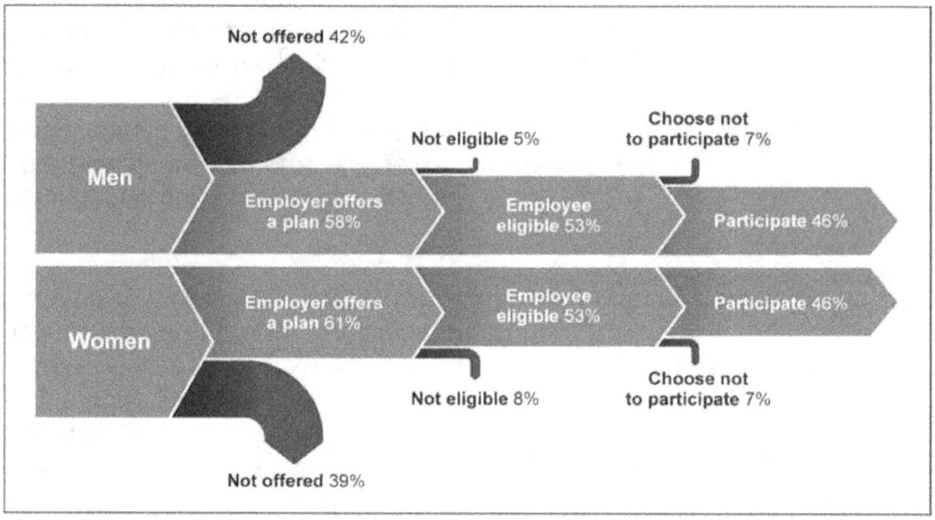

Source: GAO analysis of SIPP data.

Note: Percentage estimates in this figure have 95 percent confidence intervals that are within +/- 1 percent of the estimate itself.

Women Surpassed Men in Their Likelihood of Working for an Employer That Offers a Pension Plan

While working men and women were just as likely to have employers that offered pension plans in 1998, by 2009, these women were more likely than men to work for employers that offered pension plans (see fig. 3). This may be due to the sectors and industries in which women worked. For example, a greater proportion of women than men worked in the public and nonprofit sectors—sectors that have higher proportions of workers with access to plans offered by employers—than the for-profit sector. Women were also more likely to work in the education and health industries—industries that have higher proportions of workers with access to plans offered by employers.[29] In contrast, men had higher rates of self-employment over this period, and self-employed individuals were much less likely to have retirement plans. In addition, from 1998 to 2009, the proportion of working women and men with employers that offered pension plans declined after 2003, possibly reflecting the decline in the

---

[29]For more information on women's and men's occupations and industries and other factors associated with working for an employer that offers a plan, see appendix I.

number of employers offering DB plans.[30] Furthermore, the proportion of women working for employers offering DC plans increased, rising from 41 to 49 percent (see fig. 3). With the exception of 1998, women were more likely to work for employers that offered DC plans than were men.

Figure 3: Proportion of Working Women and Men with Employers That Offered Any Type of Pension Plan and DC Plans Specifically

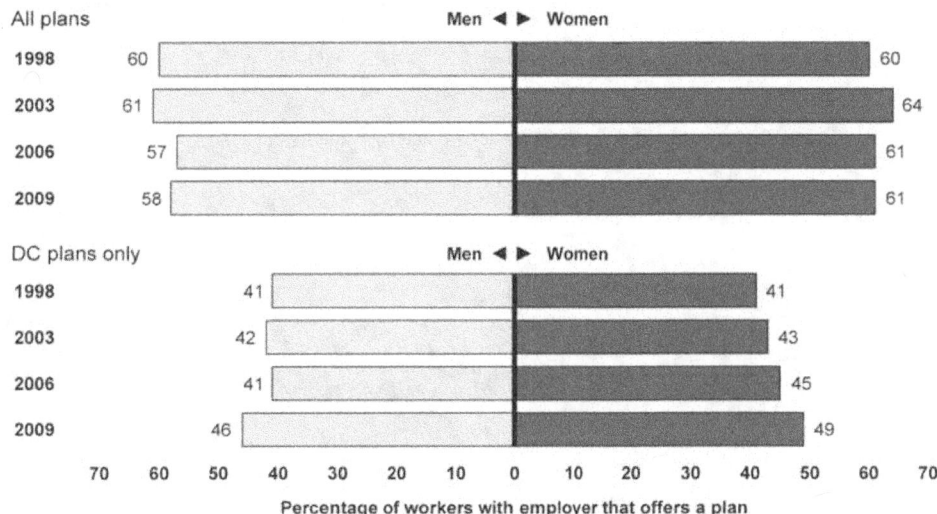

Source: GAO analysis of SIPP data.

Note: Percentage estimates in this figure have 95 percent confidence intervals that are within +/- 1 percent of the estimate itself.

---

[30]In prior work, GAO reported that net new plan formation between 2003 and 2007 had been very small (about 1 percent) and that new plan formation was offset by plan terminations or mergers. In addition, 92 percent of newly-formed plans were DC plans and were generally small, with 96 percent having fewer than 100 participants. See GAO, *Private Pensions: Some Key Features Lead to an Uneven Distribution of Benefits,* GAO-11-333 (Washington, D.C.: Mar. 30, 2011). GAO also reported that plan sponsors voluntarily terminated over 61,000 sufficiently funded single-employer DB plans from 1990 to 2006 and that a number of large employers, representing a significant portion of participants in the DB pension system, had announced their intention to freeze one or more of their DB plans. See GAO, *Defined Benefit Pensions: Plan Freezes Affect Millions of Participants and May Pose Retirement Income Challenges,* GAO-08-817 (Washington, D.C.: July 21, 2008).

GAO-12-699 Women's Retirement Security

Moreover, as shown in figure 4, while the proportion of working women with an employer that offered a DC plan increased through 2009—though not always steadily—it varied by racial and ethnic groups. White and Black women, for example, were the most likely to work for an employer that offered a plan, while Hispanic women were the least likely.[31] Interestingly, with only a few exceptions (i.e., Whites in 1998 and Asians in 2003 and 2009), the proportion of women working for an employer offering a plan was equal to or higher than that of men of the same race.

---

[31]Individuals in the White, Black, and Asian racial and ethnic categories are non-Hispanic.

Figure 4: The Proportion of Working Women and Working Men with Employers That Offered DC Pension Plans Varied, by Race

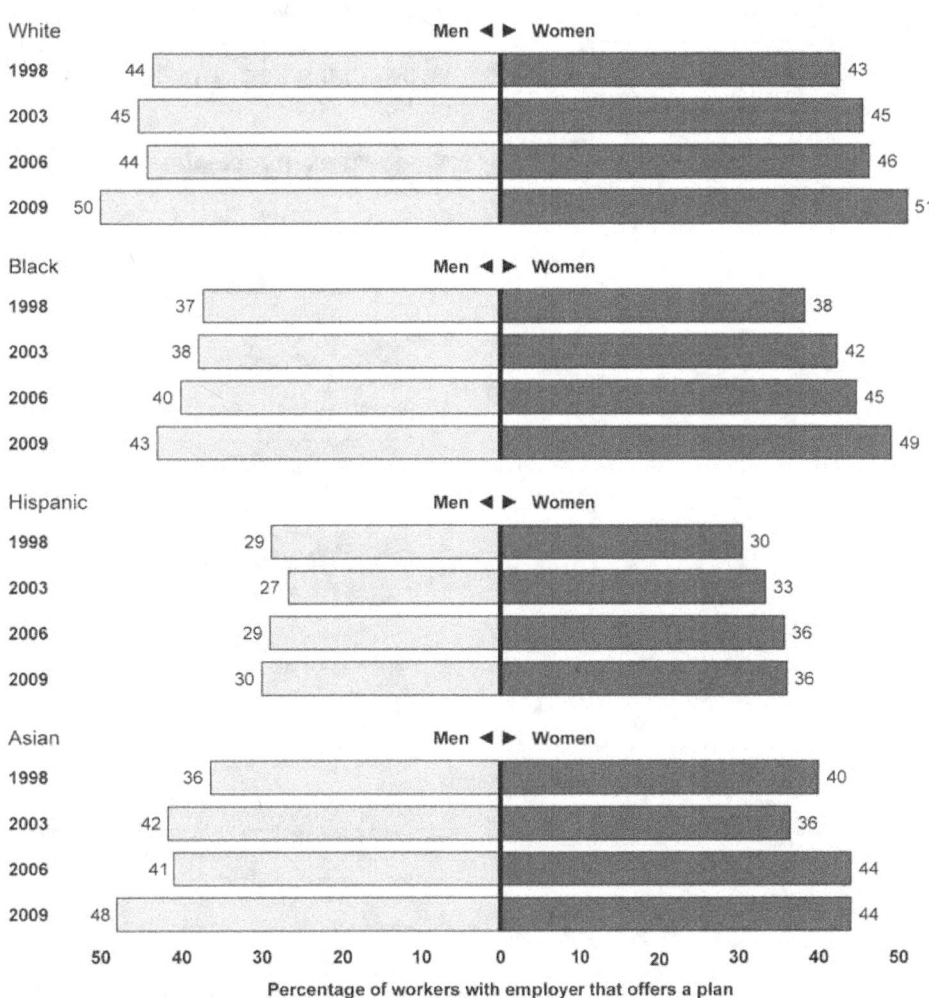

Source: GAO analysis of SIPP data.

Note: For Whites, percentage estimates in this figure have 95 percent confidence intervals that are within +/-2 percentage points or less of the estimate itself. For Blacks, Hispanics, and Asians, the 95 percent confidence intervals are within +/-3, 3 and 6 or fewer percentage points of the estimate itself respectively. For Asians, the variation by year may be due to their relatively small sample size.

Women Working for Employers Offering Plans Made Gains in Plan Eligibility

Among those working for an employer offering a pension, the vast majority of both women and men were eligible to participate in the plan, and their eligibility rates generally increased over time (see fig. 5). Moreover, women's eligibility rates increased more than men's, thereby narrowing the gap between men and women from 7 to 4 percentage points.

Figure 5: The Proportion of Working Women and Men Who Were Eligible for Their Employer's Pension Plans (among the Population Whose Employers Offered a Plan)

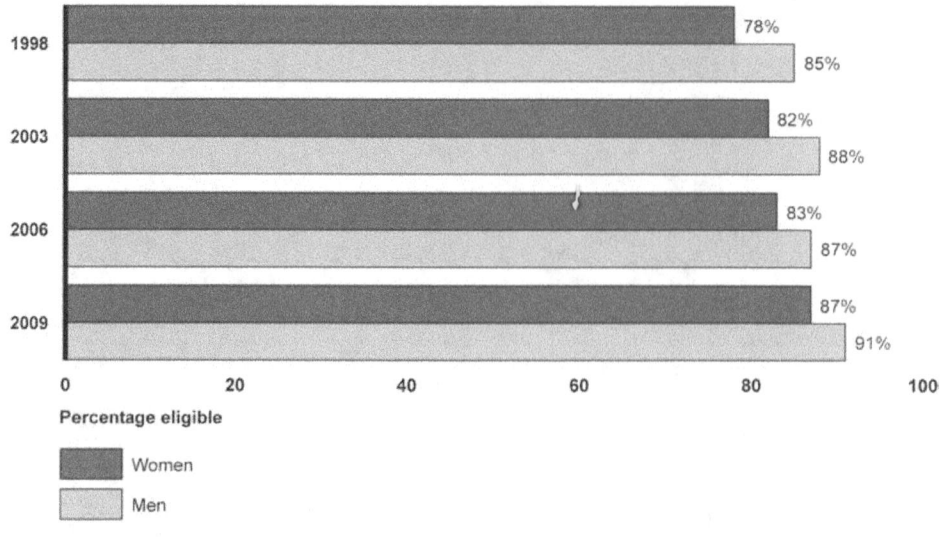

Percentage eligible

Women

Men

Source: GAO analysis of SIPP data.

Note: Percentage estimates in this figure have 95 percent confidence intervals that are within +/-2 percent or less of the estimate itself.

Of the women who were not eligible to participate in their employer's pension plan in 2009, the majority reported that they were not eligible because they did not work enough hours, weeks, or months per year at their place of employment. Correspondingly, women that worked part-time were significantly less likely to be eligible for their employer's plan, according to our analysis.[32] In contrast, men most frequently cited insufficient tenure as the reason for ineligibility.

---

[32]For more information on other factors associated with employer-plan eligibility, see appendix I.

The Gender Gap in Plan Participation Narrowed

Among those eligible to participate in their employer's pension plan, women had lower rates of participation than men, but this gap diminished over time as men's participation rates declined. Specifically, the participation rate for women in any type of plan (DB or DC) declined slightly from 87 percent in 1998 to 86 percent in 2009, while the participation rate for men declined from 91 to 87 percent (see fig. 6).

Among those eligible for DC plans, women's participation rates increased by one percentage point over the years we analyzed, while men's declined by 2 percentage points. Taken together, the gender participation gap in DC take-up rates narrowed from 4 to 1 percentage points.

Figure 6: The Proportion of Eligible Women and Men That Participated in Any Type of Employer-Sponsored Pension Plan or in DC Plans (among the Population That Was Eligible for a Plan)

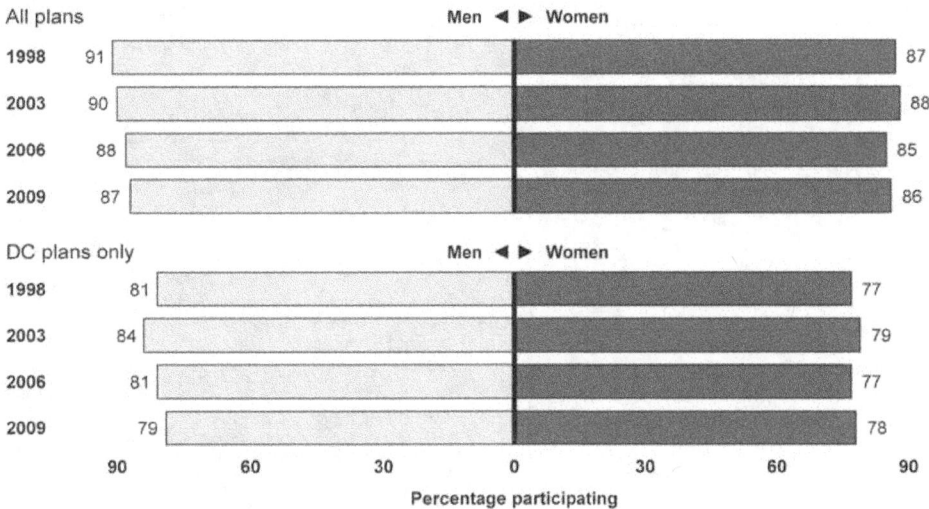

Source: GAO analysis of SIPP data.

Note: Percentage estimates in this figure have 95 percent confidence intervals that are within +/-2 percent or less of the estimate itself.

Women's participation rates in DC plans also varied by race. As shown in figure 7, White and Asian women had the highest participation rates in DC plans, ranging from 79 and 78 percent respectively in 1998 to 80 and 85 percent in 2009. Black and Hispanic women had lower participation rates, but the rate for Black women increased over time from 66 to 70 percent. With some exceptions, across all racial and ethnic groups, eligible women tended to have lower participation rates than eligible men across all 4 years.

GAO-12-699 Women's Retirement Security

Figure 7: The Proportion of Working Women and Working Men (among Those Who Were Eligible) Who Participated in Their Employer's Defined Contribution Pension Plans, by Race

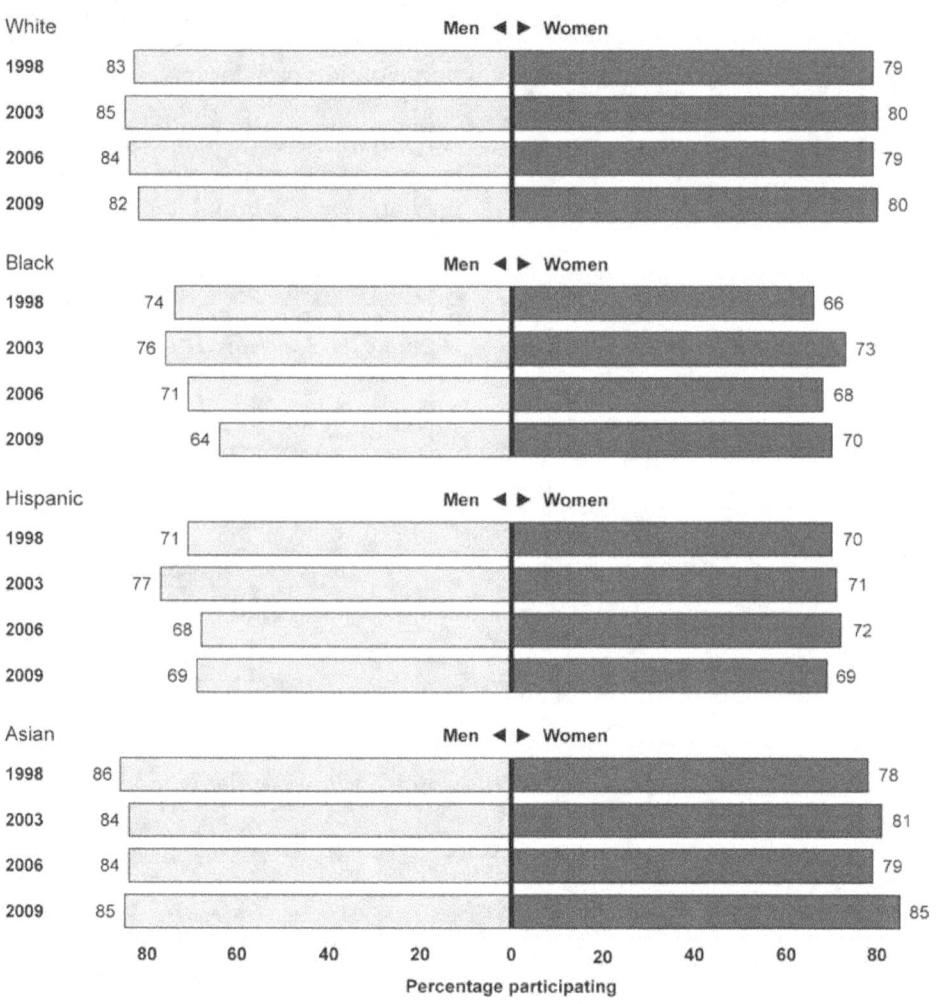

Source: GAO analysis of SIPP data.

Note: For Whites, percentage estimates in this figure have 95 percent confidence intervals that are within +/-2 percentage points or less of the estimate itself. For Blacks, Hispanics, and Asians, the 95 percent confidence intervals are within +/-5, +/-6, and +/-7 or fewer percentage points of the estimate respectively.

Several characteristics of women help to explain their lower participation rates in DC plans. For one, women had significantly lower levels of household income than men across all 4 years. Our analysis, coupled with studies conducted by outside experts, indicates that higher incomes are associated with higher rates of plan participation.[33] Further, despite women's increasing attachment to the labor force, they continue to be more likely than men to work part-time and to have less tenure—factors we and others have found to be associated with lower DC participation rates.[34] At the same time, a higher proportion of women are single-parents—a factor that we found to be negatively associated with plan participation. After accounting for these differences (and differences in other factors) between men and women, women did not have significantly lower participation rates than men in 2009.[35]

In addition to having lower rates of participation, women also contributed to their DC plans at lower levels than men. Among those reporting their contributions as shares of their salaries, women's contribution rates hovered around 6.7 percent of their salaries while men's contribution rates averaged around 7.2 percent over the years of our analysis.[36] Among those reporting their contributions in dollar amounts, women's annual contributions were consistently around 30 percent lower than men's over the study period.

---

[33]See Alicia H. Munnell, Annika Sundén, and Catherine Taylor, "What Determines 401(k) Participation and Contributions?" *Social Security Bulletin*, vol. 64, no. 3 (2001/2002). See appendix I for additional information on our modeling analyses.

[34]See Lois Shaw and Catherine Hill, *The Gender Gap in Pension Coverage: What Does the Future Hold?*, Institute for Women's Policy Research, IWPR Publication #E507 (May 15, 2001). Shaw and Hill find that hours worked per week and job tenure are positively related with participating in a pension plan.

[35]These results are consistent with those of outside researchers. For example, one study found that before controlling for differences between men and women in other factors that might affect participation, women had significantly lower participation rates than men. However, after controlling for differences between men and women, women were 6.5 percent more likely to participate in a DC plan. See Gur Huberman, Sheena S. Iyengar, and Wei Jiang, "Defined Contribution Pension Plans: Determinants of Participation and Contributions Rates," *Journal of Financial Services Research* (January 2007). For more information on other factors associated with employer-plan participation, see appendix I.

[36]These estimates of contribution levels are consistent with estimates (for both men and women combined) from other studies using recent SIPP data. See, for example, "Retirement Plan Participation: Survey of Income and Program Participation (SIPP) Data, 2009" *Employee Benefit Research Institute Notes*, vol. 31, no.11 (November 2010): 2.

While Income Composition Changed Only Slightly for Women Age 65 and Over, They Continue to Have Less Retirement Income Than Men

The composition of women's and men's retirement income did not vary greatly over the last decade despite changes in the economy and pension system, largely because their main income sources—Social Security and DB plans—were shielded from fluctuations in the financial market. However, women, especially widows and those 80 years and over, depended on Social Security benefits for a larger percentage of their income than men. In contrast, women received a lower share of their income from earnings than men. Women age 65 and over also had less retirement income on average and higher rates of poverty than men in that age group. Specifically, for the population age 65 and over, women's median income was approximately 25 percent lower than men in the same age group for all years.[37] Moreover, women in this age group were nearly twice as likely to be living in poverty than men.

The Composition of Income for Women and Men Age 65 and Over Did Not Fluctuate Greatly Despite Changes in the Economy and Pension System

The composition of household income for women and men age 65 and over fluctuated only slightly from 1998 to 2010, despite changes in the economy and the pension system (see fig. 8). The composition of household income did not fluctuate drastically largely because Social Security and DB benefits comprised nearly three-quarters of household income for women and slightly less (around 70 percent) for men, providing them with guaranteed monthly income for life. Women tended to receive a higher proportion of household income from Social Security. In fact, in 2010, 16 percent of women age 65 and over depended solely on Social Security for income compared to 12 percent of men. At the same time, the share of income from earnings increased slightly for men and women, but was consistently lower for women than for men. Furthermore, the share of income from DC plans was very low (1 to 2 percent) across the entire period for both men and women. This is due to the fact that the lion's share of people age 65 and over did not report receiving any income from regular distributions from DC plans.[38]

---

[37]For the analysis in this section, we used SIPP data from 1998, 2003, 2006, and 2010. See appendix I for more details on the data and our analyses.

[38]This may be due to the fact that retirees tend to withdraw funds from DC accounts irregularly, instead of annuitizing. To the extent that nonregular (lump sum) distributions comprise a significant portion of income, our estimates of income shares from other sources, such as Social Security, might be overstated. However, because of the irregularity of these lump sum distributions, it is difficult to observe them with household survey data because surveys generally measure income only at a particular point in time.

Figure 8: The Composition of Household Income for Women and Men Age 65 and Over Did Not Fluctuate Greatly Over Time

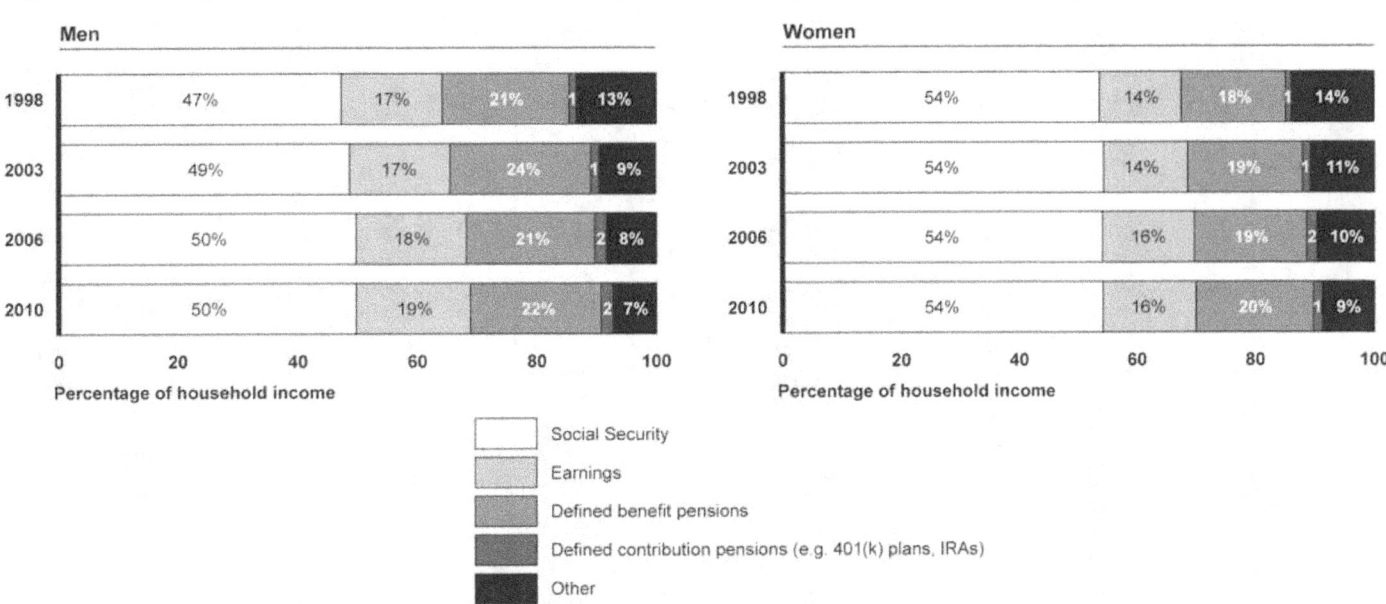

Men

1998	47%	17%	21% 1	13%
2003	49%	17%	24% 1	9%
2006	50%	18%	21% 2	8%
2010	50%	19%	22% 2	7%

0   20   40   60   80   100
Percentage of household income

Women

1998	54%	14%	18% 1	14%
2003	54%	14%	19% 1	11%
2006	54%	16%	19% 2	10%
2010	54%	16%	20% 1	9%

0   20   40   60   80   100
Percentage of household income

- Social Security
- Earnings
- Defined benefit pensions
- Defined contribution pensions (e.g. 401(k) plans, IRAs)
- Other

Source: GAO analysis of SIPP data.

Notes: Estimates for men and women include spousal income. The category for income from defined contribution pensions reflects total household distributions from IRAs, as well as 401(k) pension plans and similar defined contribution pension plans. Nonregular (lump sum) withdrawals from IRA and 401(k) plans are not included. The "other" category includes income from cash public assistance and property income including interest, dividends, rent and royalties. Percentages may not add to 100% due to rounding. Percentages are based on household incomes for each source including zero values. Percentage estimates of the income shares from Social Security, earnings, defined benefit pension, and defined contribution pensions have 95 percent confidence intervals that are within +/- 2.5 percent of the estimate itself. For information on how these percentages were estimated, see appendix I.

As shown in figures 9 to 11, in 2010, the composition of household income for individuals age 65 and over also varied by demographic group. Among marital-status categories, widowed women depended on Social Security benefits for a larger percentage of their income (58 percent) than other women (see fig. 9). In fact, about 21 percent of all widowed women depended on Social Security as their sole source of income. Separated women and men received higher shares of income from earnings, and married women and men received relatively higher shares of their income from DB plans.

GAO-12-699 Women's Retirement Security

Figure 9: Differences in the Composition of Household Income for Women and Men Age 65 and Over, by Marital Status, 2010

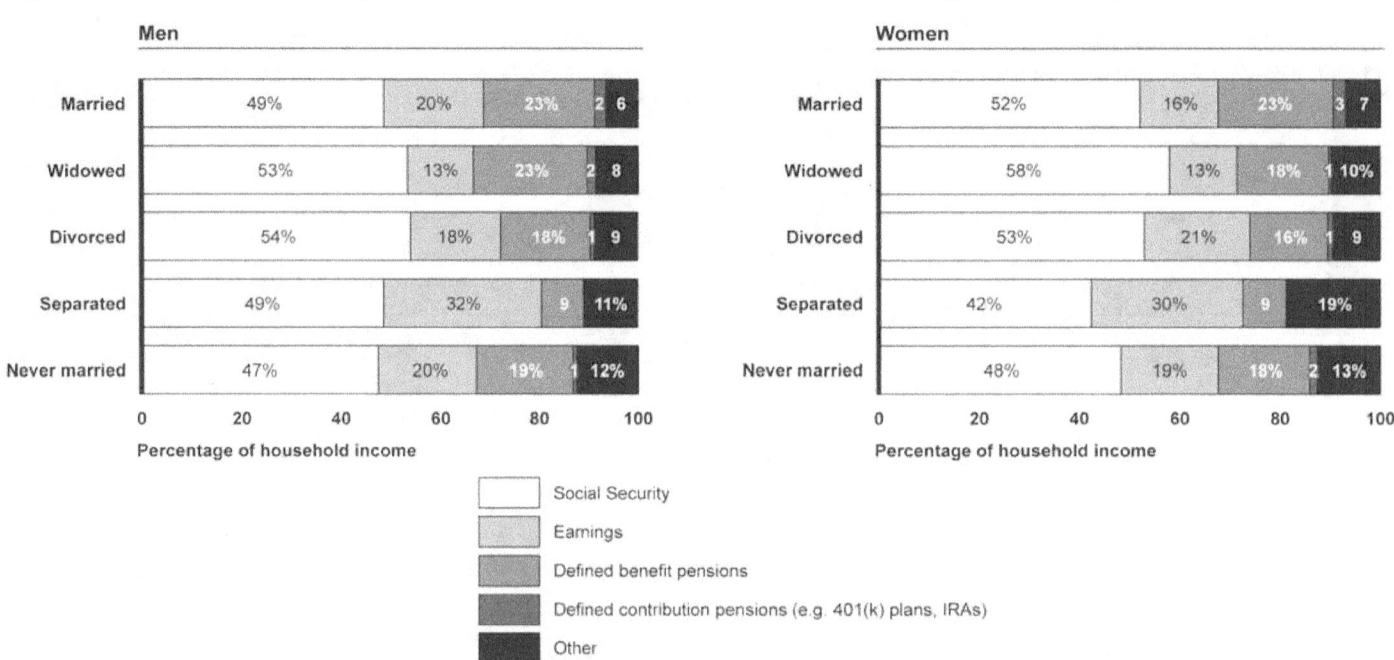

Source: GAO analysis of SIPP data.

Notes: In the category for married individuals, estimates for men and women include spousal income. The category for income from defined contribution pensions reflects total household distributions from IRAs, as well as 401(k) and similar defined contribution pension plans. Nonregular (lump sum) withdrawals are not included. The "other" category includes income cash public assistance and property income including interest, dividends, rent and royalties. Percentages may not add to 100% due to rounding. Percentage estimates of the income shares from Social Security have 95 percent confidence intervals that are within +/-2, +/-3, +/-4, +/-10 and +/-6 percent of the estimate itself for married, widowed, divorced, separated and never married individuals respectively. Percentage estimates of the income shares from earnings have 95 percent confidence intervals that are within +/-2, +/-2, +/-3, +/-11 and +/-6 percent of the estimate itself for married, widowed, divorced, separated and never married individuals respectively. Percentage estimates of the income shares from defined benefit plans have 95 percent confidence intervals that are within +/-2, +/-3, +/-3, +/-7 and +/-5 percent of the estimate itself for married, widowed, divorced, separated and never married individuals respectively. Percentage estimates of the income shares from defined contribution plans have 95 percent confidence intervals that are within +/- 2 percent of the estimate itself for all marital status categories.

As shown in figure 10, among different age groups, women age 80 and over received the highest share of their income from Social Security (61 percent). In fact, about 20 percent of them depended on Social Security for their sole source of income. Men in the youngest age category (65 to 69) received a higher share of their income from earnings (31 percent) relative to other groups, while individuals in the oldest age categories received the smallest share of income from earnings, likely reflecting the declining ability to work at older ages.

GAO-12-699 Women's Retirement Security

Figure 10: Differences in the Composition of Household Income for Women and Men Age 65 and Over, by Age Group, 2010

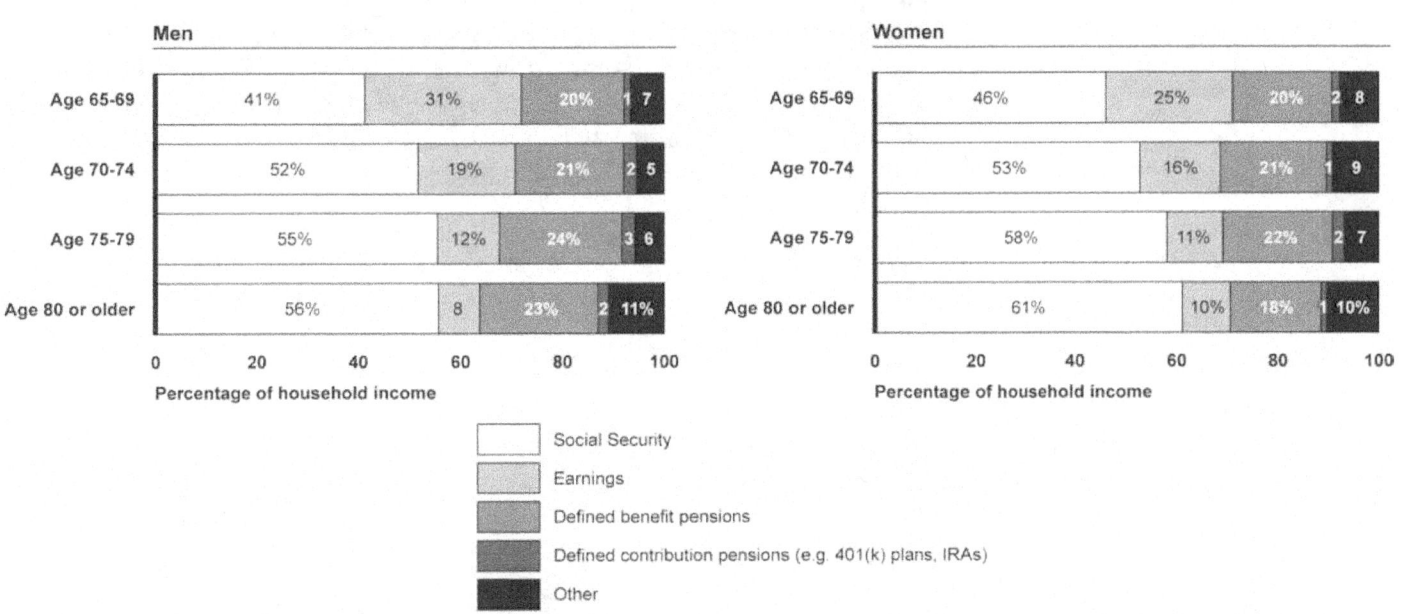

Source: GAO analysis of SIPP data.

Notes: Estimates for men and women include spousal income. The category for income from defined contr bution pensions reflects total household distributions from IRAs, as well as 401(k) and similar defined contribution pension plans. Nonregular (lump sum) withdrawals are not included. The "other" category includes income from cash public assistance and property income including interest, dividends, rent and royalties. Percentages may not add to 100 percent due to rounding. Percentage estimates of the income shares from Social Security have 95 percent confidence intervals that are within +/-2, +/-4, +/-3, and +/-2 percent of the estimate itself for individuals in the 65-69, 70-74, 75-79, and 80+ age categories respectively. Percentage estimates of the income shares from earnings have 95 percent confidence intervals that are within +/-2 percent of the estimate itself for individuals in all age categories respectively. Percentage estimates of the income shares from defined benefit pension plans have 95 percent confidence intervals that are within +/-2, +/-2, +/-2, and +/-4 percent of the estimate itself for individuals in the 65-69, 70-74, 75-79, and 80+ age categories respectively. Percentage estimates of the income shares from defined contribution pension plans have 95 percent confidence intervals that are within +/-0.5, +/-3, +/-1, and +/-1 percent of the estimate itself for individuals in the 65-69, 70-74, 75-79, and 80+ age categories respectively.

Finally, among racial and ethnic groups, White and Black women and men age 65 and over received the highest share of income from Social Security (see fig. 11). In contrast, Asians and Hispanics tended to receive a lower share of their incomes from Social Security.[39] Asian men and women received a disproportionately higher share of income from earnings relative to other racial and ethnic categories. White and Black women and men received higher shares of income from DB plans, compared to Hispanics and Asians.

---

[39]In "Racial and Ethnic Differences in Women's Retirement Security," *Journal of Women, Politics & Policy,* 30 (2009): 141-171, Sunhwa Lee also notes that Social Security is the most common source of retirement income and that differences in immigrant status do not entirely account for the lower rates of Social Security receipt among Hispanics and Asians. Maya Rockeymoore and Meizhu Lui highlight that Hispanics are disproportionately represented in job categories that were previously excluded from the Social Security program, such as agricultural and household workers. They point out that, although these job categories are now covered, earnings in these categories might not be recorded accurately in Social Security tax payment records, which could lead to lower payments and therefore a lower share of income from Social Security. See Maya M. Rockeymoore and Meizhu Lui, *Plan for a New Future: The Impact of Social Security Reform on People of Color* (Washington, D.C.: Commission to Modernize Social Security, 2011).

Figure 11: Differences in the Composition of Household Income for Women and Men Age 65 and Over, by Race and Ethnicity, 2010

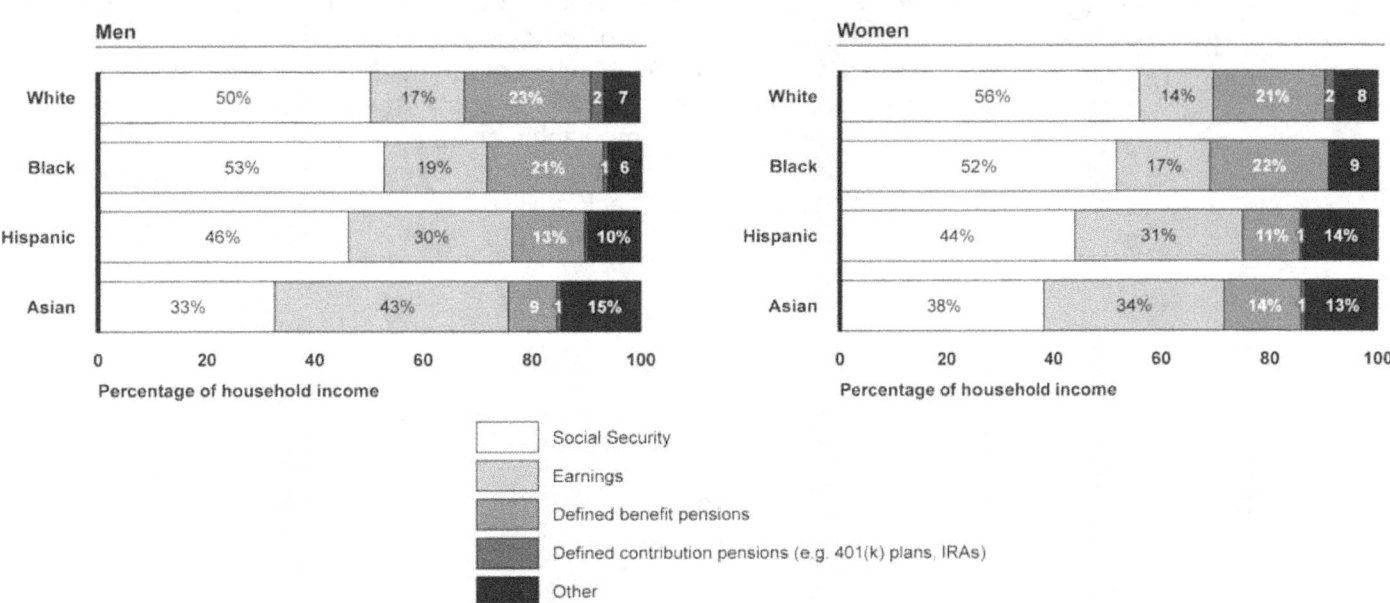

Source: GAO analysis of SIPP data.

Notes: Estimates for men and women include spousal income. The category for income from defined contribution pensions reflects total household distributions from IRAs, as well as 401(k) and similar defined contribution pension plans. Nonregular (lump sum) withdrawals are not included. The "other" category includes income from cash public assistance and property income including interest, dividends, rent and royalties. Percentages may not add to 100 percent due to rounding. The size of the 95 percent confidence intervals for estimates presented in this figure varies by racial/ethnic category. Percentage estimates of the income shares from Social Security have 95 percent confidence intervals that are within +/-2, +/-4, +/-5, and +/-6 percent of the estimate itself for White, Black, Hispanic, and Asian individuals respectively. Percentage estimates of the income shares from earnings have 95 percent confidence intervals that are within +/-1, +/-3, +/-5, and +/-7 percent of the estimate itself for White, Black, Hispanic, and Asian individuals respectively. Percentage estimates of the income shares from defined benefit plans have 95 percent confidence intervals that are within +/-2, +/-3, +/-3, and +/-7 percent of the estimate itself for White, Black, Hispanic, and Asian individuals respectively. Percentage estimates of the income shares from defined contribution plans have 95 percent confidence intervals that are within +/-1 percent for all the racial and ethnic categories.

GAO-12-699 Women's Retirement Security

Median Household Income for Women Age 65 and Over Was 25 Percent Lower Than Men's

Women age 65 and over had consistently lower median incomes than men across age and most race groups over time.[40] Over the last decade, the median incomes of women age 65 and over were approximately 25 percent lower than their male counterparts. Median incomes, did, however, vary by demographic category (see fig. 12). Demographic groups with the lowest median incomes included women who were either unmarried—especially those who had been separated or never married—over the age-of 80, or Black or Hispanic.

---

[40]We used SIPP data to analyze household income among individuals 65 and over from 1998 to 2010.

Figure 12: Median Household Incomes in 2010 for Individuals 65 and Over by Age Group

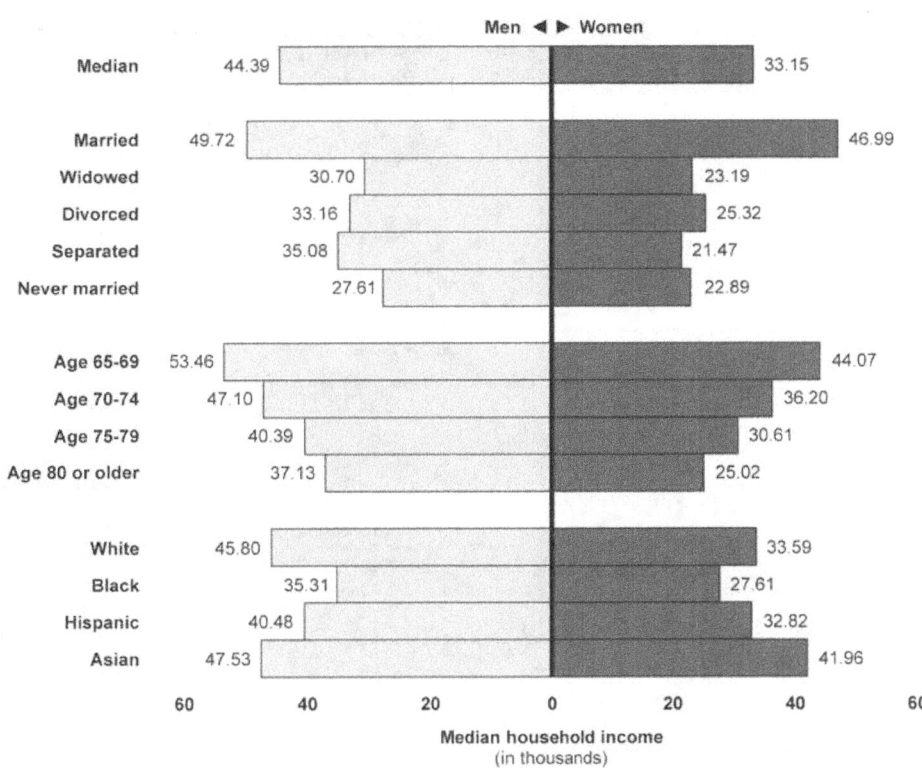

Men ◀ ▶ Women

	Men	Women
Median	44.39	33.15
Married	49.72	46.99
Widowed	30.70	23.19
Divorced	33.16	25.32
Separated	35.08	21.47
Never married	27.61	22.89
Age 65-69	53.46	44.07
Age 70-74	47.10	36.20
Age 75-79	40.39	30.61
Age 80 or older	37.13	25.02
White	45.80	33.59
Black	35.31	27.61
Hispanic	40.48	32.82
Asian	47.53	41.96

Median household income
(in thousands)

Source: GAO analysis of SIPP data.

Notes: Estimates for men and women include spousal income. Estimates of median incomes have 95 percent confidence intervals that are within +/-$900 for women and +/-$1,200 for men in the entire U.S., +/-$1,600 for married women, +/-$1,000 for widowed women, +/-$1,900 for divorced women, +/-$5,200 for separated women, +/-$4,000 for never married women, +/-$1,800 for married men, +/-$2,000 for widowed men, +/-$4,100 for divorced men, +/- $8,000 for separated men, +/-$3,500 for never married men, +/-$1,800 for women ages 65-69, +/-1,700 for woman age ages 70-74, +/-$2,100 for women ages 75-79, +/-$900 for women 80 and older, +/-$2,700 for men ages 65-69, +/-$2,300 for men ages 70-74 and 75-79, +/-$2,200 for men 80 and over, +/-$1,000 for White women, +/-$1,400 for Black women, +/- $4,300 for Hispanic women, +/-$5,000 for Asian women, +/-$1,400 for White men, +/-$2,900 for Black men, +/-$5,300 for Hispanic men, and +/-$7,100 for Asian men.

In addition, a greater proportion of women age 65 and over lived in households with incomes below the poverty line than men in the same age group. Consistent with their relatively lower median incomes, the demographic groups with the highest poverty rates were women who were not married, over the age of 80, or non-White (see fig. 13).[41] In contrast, married people and White men had the lowest poverty rates.

Figure 13: Poverty Rates by Demographic Categories in 2010 for Women and Men Age 65 and Over

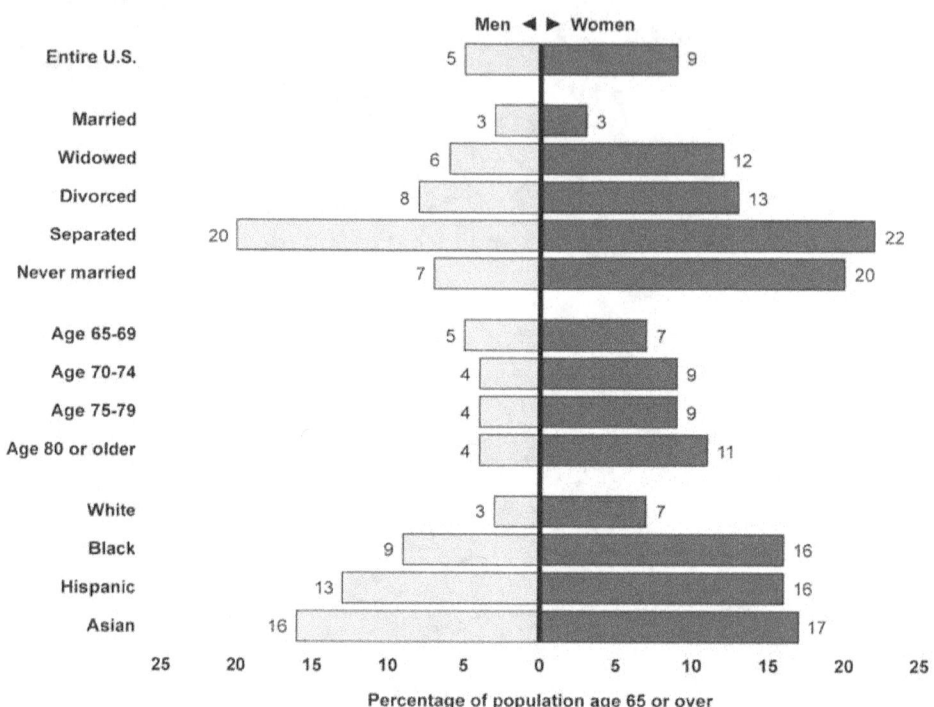

Men ◄ ► Women

Category	Men	Women
Entire U.S.	5	9
Married	3	3
Widowed	6	12
Divorced	8	13
Separated	20	22
Never married	7	20
Age 65-69	5	7
Age 70-74	4	9
Age 75-79	4	9
Age 80 or older	4	11
White	3	7
Black	9	16
Hispanic	13	16
Asian	16	17

Percentage of population age 65 or over

Source: GAO analysis of SIPP data.

Note: Estimates for men and women include spousal income. Percentage estimates of poverty rates have 95 percent confidence intervals that are within +/-1 percent for the category for the entire U.S.; +/-1 percent for married, +/-2 percent for widowed, +/-3 percent for divorced, +/-12 percent for separated, and +/-6 percent for never married individuals; +/-2 percent for all age-categories; +/-1 percent for Whites, +/-4 percent for Blacks, +/-5 percent for Hispanics, and +/-8 percent for Asians.

[41]Lee (2009) and Rockeymoore, et al. (2011) find similar results regarding higher poverty rates among unmarried and non-White women.

GAO-12-699 Women's Retirement Security

Divorce, Widowhood, and Unemployment Had a Detrimental Effect on Older Women's Income Security

When women nearing or in retirement—women over age 50—became divorced, widowed or unemployed, the effects on their households' total assets and income were detrimental, according to our analysis (see table 1).[42] Further, divorce and widowhood had more pronounced effects for women than for men. These effects may be contributing to elderly women's higher poverty rates and lower levels of income compared to men's. We also found, not surprisingly, that a decline in health after age 50 had a negative effect on household assets and income.[43] Lastly, we also examined the effect of caring for elderly parents on income and assets, but we did not find statistically significant negative relationships. All of these effects may not be generalizable to younger cohorts as women's labor force participation and, correspondingly, their assets and income, have changed over the last several decades.[44]

---

[42]We estimated these effects using fixed-effects panel regressions. We used all available years of HRS data, from 1992 up through the early release data for 2010. Because the HRS tracks individuals over time, we were able to estimate the percent change in household assets and household income that occurs for an individual after a life event, relative to an individual that did not experience that life event, but also became older. In this way, we were able to isolate the effect of the life event from other factors. We analyzed the effect of each event individually. If a woman were to experience multiple events simultaneously, such as becoming divorced and unemployed, the effects on her household assets and income could be even larger. For more details on our methodology and results, including standard errors, see appendix I.

[43]For our analysis, we used a user-friendly longitudinal dataset created by RAND, a research organization. For total household assets, we used RAND's variable that includes all household assets except for secondary residences. For income, we used RAND's total household income variable. For more information on the RAND dataset, see appendix I.

[44]Respondents in our sample were born prior to 1954; the HRS grouped these individuals into five generational cohorts. In addition, these analyses did not adjust for the size of the household, but show the effect on total household income and assets for a person experiencing the event. When we adjusted our models for household size, we found smaller effects for divorce and widowhood, but these effects were still significant. See appendix I for more information.

Table 1: Estimated Effects of Life Events on Household Assets and Income by Gender

Percent change

	Total household assets		Total household income	
	Women	**Men**	**Women**	**Men**
Became divorced or separated	-41[a]	-39[a]	-41[a,b]	-23[a,b]
Became widowed	-32[a,b]	-27[a,b]	-37[a,b]	-22[a,b]
Became unemployed	-7[a]	-7[a]	-9[a]	-7[a]
Health declined	-8[a]	-10[a]	-4[a]	-3[a]
Helped parents financially	3[a]	3[a]	6[a]	7[a]
Helped parents with daily activities	1	1	2[a]	2[a]

Source: GAO analysis of HRS data.

Notes: We used fixed-effects regression models to estimate the percent change in total household assets and income that occurs for an individual after a life event, relative to an individual that did not experience that life event. Total assets and income for the household were applied to each individual in the household. The estimated effects represent the average percent difference in household assets and income between all survey periods in which the household does experience an event and all survey periods in which the household does not experience an event. The event may have occurred in any year after the household entered the survey. For more details on the models, see appendix I.

[a]Estimate is significantly different from zero.

[b]Difference between women and men is statistically significant.

Became Divorced or Separated after Age 50

As shown in figure 14, the effects of divorce or separation after age 50 had substantial, negative effects on women's total household assets and income. For both women and men, assets fell by about 40 percent with a divorce or separation.[45] The effects were less substantial for those living in households where at least one member was age 65 or over, but these women and men still lost about one-third of their total assets. The effects for income were more pronounced for women than for men. Women's income fell by 41 percent, nearly twice that of men's (23 percent). The effects were largest for women living in households where all members

---

[45]Our estimated effects represent the average percent difference in household assets and income between all survey periods in which the household does experience an event and all survey periods in which the household does not experience an event.

GAO-12-699 Women's Retirement Security

were age 64 or younger; for these women, income fell by 44 percent.[46] However, while divorce had very detrimental effects, we found that, for women ages 51 and over, divorce or separation was less prevalent than widowhood. Specifically, for those age 85 and over in our sample, 4 percent of women and 2 percent of men had been divorced or separated.[47]

---

[46]Researchers have hypothesized that the drop in assets is due to households saving their assets for a rainy day and are primarily drawn down at the time of precipitating shocks, such as divorce. See James M. Poterba, Steven F. Venti, and David A. Wise, *Family Status Transitions, Latent Health, and the Post-Retirement Evolution of Assets*, NBER Working Paper 15789, issued in February 2010. Also, Wilmoth and Koso hypothesize that the mechanisms that systematically allocate wealth when a marriage ends are more effective at maintaining wealth for those who are widowed compared to those who are divorced. They conclude that divorce should be more detrimental to long-term wealth accumulation than widowhood. See Janet Wilmoth and Gregor Koso, "Does Marital History Matter? Marital Status and Wealth Outcomes Among Preretirement Adults," *Journal of Marriage and Family*, vol. 64, no. 1 (2002).

[47]Further, some of these women and men could have been divorced prior to entering our sample.

Figure 14: Estimated Effects of Divorce and Separation on Total Household Assets and Income

Change in total household assets

Change in total household income

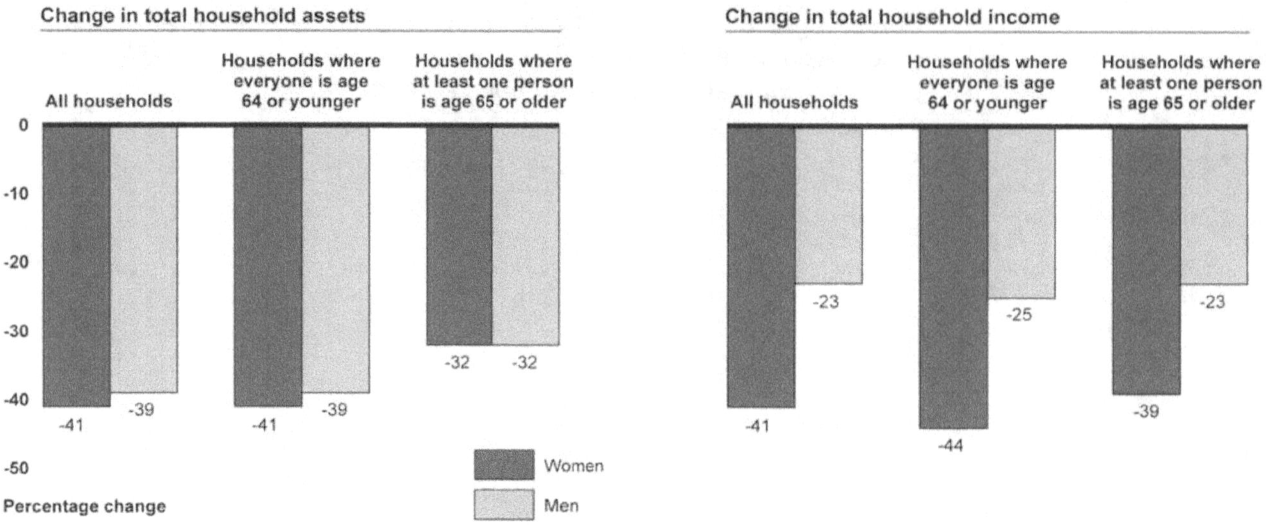

Source: GAO analysis of HRS data.

Notes: All estimates in this figure have 95 percent confidence intervals within +/-8 percentage points of the estimate itself. For statistical comparisons of the estimates across different groups, see appendix I. We used fixed-effects regression models to estimate the percent change in total household assets and income that occurs for an individual after a life event, relative to an individual that did not experience that life event. Total assets and income for the household were applied to each individual in the household. The estimated effects represent the average percent difference in household assets and income between all survey periods in which the household does experience an event and all survey periods in which the household does not experience an event. The event may have occurred in any year after the household entered the survey. For more details on the models, see appendix I.

Became Widowed after Age 50

Not only did women's total household assets and income decline substantially with widowhood, but the effects were more pronounced for women than for men (see fig. 15). For example, while men's income fell 22 percent after widowerhood, women's income fell by an even greater amount—37 percent. The effects were larger for women living in younger households than women living in older households. Specifically, women in households where all members were age 64 or younger experienced a

31 percent decrease in assets and a 47 percent decrease in income.[48] Adding to these effects, widowhood was a much more common experience for women than men in our sample. In fact, women were at least twice as likely as men to become widowed between any two survey periods. Consequently, 70 percent of women age 85 and over were widowed compared to only 24 percent of men age 85 and over.

---

[48]A widow's assets may be depleted by medical and other expenses incurred prior to the death of her spouse. See Kathleen McGarry and Robert F. Schoeni, "Medicare Gaps and Widow Poverty," *Social Security Bulletin*, vol. 66, no. 1 (2005). In addition, women's income may fall after widowhood if their husbands did not elect to take the husband's pension benefits in the form of a joint and survivor benefit. See Karen C. Holden and Angela Fontes, "Economic Security in Retirement: How Changes in Employment and Marriage Have Altered Retirement-Related Economic Risks for Women," *Journal of Women, Politics & Policy*, vol. 30, no. 2-3 (2009).

Figure 15: Estimated Effects of Widowhood on Total Household Assets and Income

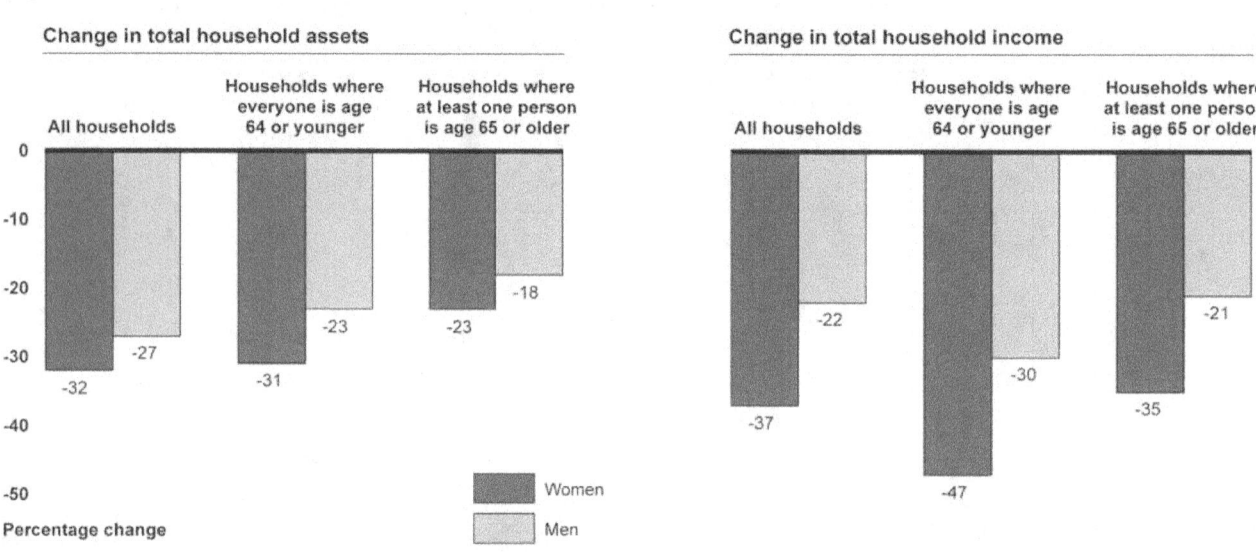

Source: GAO analysis of HRS data.

Notes: Because widows appear much more often in households where at least one person is over the age of 65 than in households where everyone is age 64 or younger, part of the overall effect is likely a comparison of the household's assets over time. This explains why the effect for the larger population is larger than the effect for each of the groups. Estimates for the "all households" and "households where at least one person is age 65 or older" categories have 95 percent confidence intervals within +/-5 percentage points of the estimate itself. Estimates for the "households where everyone is age 64 or younger" category have 95 percent confidence intervals within +/-10 percentage points of the estimate itself. For statistical comparisons of the estimates across different groups, see appendix I. We used fixed-effects regression models to estimate the percent change in total household assets and income that occurs for an individual after a life event, relative to an individual that did not experience that life event. Total assets and income for the household were applied to each individual in the household. The estimated effects represent the average percent difference in household assets and income between all survey periods in which the household does experience an event and all survey periods in which the household does not experience an event. The event may have occurred in any year after the household entered the survey. For more details on the models, see appendix I.

Became Unemployed after Age 50

Similar to becoming widowed, unemployment had negative effects on total household assets and income, although the effects were similar for women and men (see fig. 16).[49] Women and men saw their assets and income decline by about 7 to 9 percent. The effects on income were most acute for households where at least one member of the household was age 65 or over. For these households, men's assets fell by 14 percent

---

[49]We defined unemployment as being out of work and actively looking for a job.

GAO-12-699 Women's Retirement Security

and their income fell by 12 percent. For women, there was not a significant decline in assets but their income fell by 13 percent. In addition, older workers may have difficulty finding another job.[50] However, unemployment was not very prevalent in the HRS sample, in part because many survey respondents were retired.[51] On average, only 1 percent of men and women reported being out of work and actively looking for a job. For men and women ages 51 to 64, this percentage rose slightly to 2 percent.

Figure 16: Estimated Effects of Unemployment on Total Household Assets and Income

Source: GAO analysis of HRS data.

Notes: Estimates for the "all households" and "households where everyone is age 64 or younger" categories have 95 percent confidence intervals within +/-6 percentage points of the estimate itself. Estimates for the "households where at least one member is age 65 or older" category have 95 percent confidence intervals within +/-15 percentage points of the estimate itself. For statistical comparisons of the estimates across different groups, see appendix I. We used fixed-effects regression models to estimate the percent change in total household assets and income that occurs for an individual after a life event, relative to an individual that did not experience that life event. Total assets and income for the household were applied to each individual in the household. The estimated effects represent the average percent difference in household assets and income between all survey periods in which the household does experience an event and all survey periods in which the household does not experience an event. The event may have occurred in any year after the household entered the survey. For more details on the models, see appendix I.

[50]We have previously reported that older workers generally have longer spells of unemployment than younger workers and that older workers report facing difficulties finding new jobs after being laid off. See GAO-12-445.

[51]When individuals enter the HRS sample, they are between the ages of 51 and 61. However, because this is a longitudinal study, all the survey members age over time. For example, someone who was age 61 at the time of the first HRS survey in 1992 was age 79 in 2010.

Health Declined after Age 50

As shown in figure 17, a decline in self-reported health status also had negative effects on total household income and assets, although to a lesser degree than widowhood, divorce, and unemployment. For all households in our sample, income fell by 4 percent for women and 3 percent for men when self-reported health status changed from excellent, very good or good to fair or poor.[52] The effects of a decline in health on assets varied by household type. The differences between women and men were the largest for younger households, where all members were age 64 or younger. For example, the loss of assets was greater for men (13 percent) compared to women (5 percent).[53]

Figure 17: Estimated Effects of a Decline in Health on Total Household Assets and Income

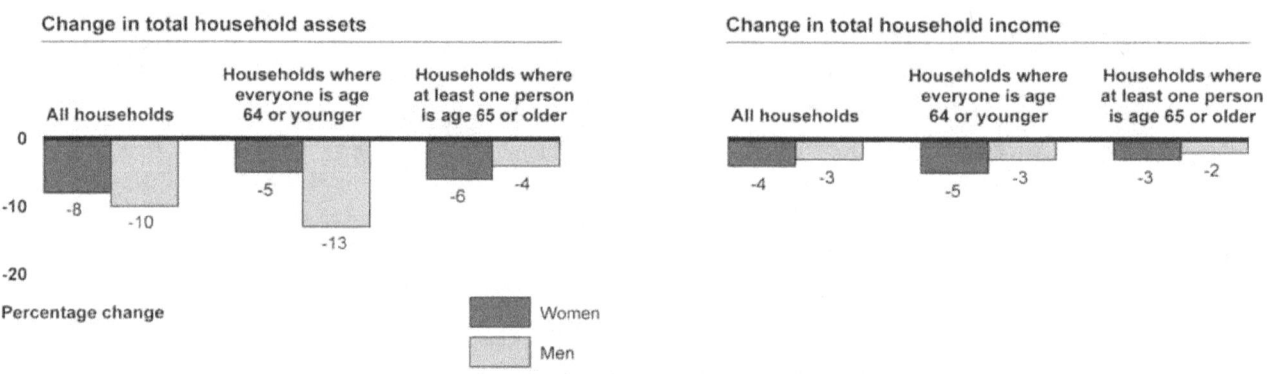

Source: GAO analysis of HRS data.

Notes: All estimates in this figure have 95 percent confidence intervals within +/-3 percentage points of the estimate itself. For statistical comparisons of the estimates across different groups, see appendix I. We used fixed-effects regression models to estimate the percent change in total household assets and income that occurs for an individual after a life event, relative to an individual that did not experience that life event. Total assets and income for the household were applied to each individual in the household. The estimated effects represent the average percent difference in household assets and income between all survey periods in which the household does experience an event and all survey periods in which the household does not experience an event. The event may have occurred in any year after the household entered the survey. For more details on the models, see appendix I.

[52]This difference between women and men is not statistically significant.

[53]Health care costs may deplete elderly individuals' resources. See McGarry and Schoeni (2005). Also see Richard W. Johnson, Gordon B.T. Mermin, and Cori E. Uccello, *When the Nest Egg Cracks: Financial Consequences of Health Problems, Marital Status Changes, and Job Layoffs at Older Ages* (Urban Institute: January 2006).

Although the effects of a decline in health were smaller than the effects of some of the other life events in our analysis, more individuals experienced this event than any other. Almost 30 percent of individuals ages 65 to 84 reported being in poor health (see table 2). For individuals ages 85 and over, 40 percent reported being in poor health. Interestingly, as shown in table 2, women and men suffered from poor health at similar rates across age categories. Further, we found that, between any two HRS surveys, about 2 percent of both women and men reported entering a period of poor health.

Table 2: Percent of Women and Men Reporting Their Health Is Poor Is Similar across Age Groups

Percent reporting their health is poor

	Women	Men
Ages 51-64	21	20
Ages 65-84	28	28
Ages 85 and over	40	40

Source: GAO analysis of HRS data.

Lastly, we found that providing elderly parents with financial assistance or helping parents with basic activities of daily living (i.e., bathing, dressing, and eating) had a slightly positive effect on household assets and income. However, often these effects were not significantly different from zero, possibly because of limitations in our data and methods.[54] In addition, we found that only a small percentage of the sample provided these types of assistance to their parents. Also, women and men age 51 through 64 were much more likely to provide assistance than women and men age 65 and over. But, as the baby boomers age, more children may be called upon to help their parents financially or with basic activities.

---

[54]Although the fixed-effects method offers several advantages over other regression methods, it also has limitations that may affect our estimates. For example, while the fixed-effects method controls for all characteristics within a household that do not change over time, it is possible that the relationship between providing care for parents and household assets changes over time and works in multiple directions. For example, if a household sees an increase in the value of its assets, it may decide to use some of this new wealth to finance care for elderly parents. However, using these assets causes total household assets to fall. The fixed-effects method cannot control for these simultaneous effects and, thus, the two effects may cancel each other out. For more information on our analysis of the effects of providing help to elderly parents and an analysis describing the individuals who provided care to parents, see appendix I.

Existing Policy Options Could Address Retirement Security Issues Facing Women

Through our interviews with experts and our literature review, we found that a range of existing policy options could help improve retirement income security for women.[55] Our analysis focuses on how women would be affected by these policy options. While each of these options would be available for both women and men, they could help address some of the specific challenges women face in ensuring a secure retirement. For example, some options would expand the use of existing tax incentives, encouraging women to save more. Another set of options would expand access to and strengthen spousal protections for retirement savings. These options could increase women's retirement savings and preserve their retirement income if they become divorced or widowed. Other sets of options could motivate women nearing retirement to work longer and save more, ensure lifetime retirement income, or enhance benefit adequacy. These options could help shield women from the effects of divorce, widowhood, and unemployment and decrease their risk of living in poverty.

All of the options have cost implications that would need to be considered prior to implementation. Moreover, as with federal spending programs, any option that results in reduced or deferred federal tax revenue may require an offset, such as raising revenue elsewhere or cutting spending. While the federal government could bear some of these costs, workers and plan sponsors could be responsible for others. Also, although some of the options could have positive effects on women on their own, there could be an offsetting effect. If the plan sponsor, for example, is responsible for the increased cost of sponsorship and makes changes to the plan to offset those increased costs, women may not ultimately benefit from the policy option. Lastly, some of these changes may require legislative changes.

---

[55]To identify and analyze policy options that could enhance women's retirement security, we conducted an extensive literature review and interviewed a range of experts. To ensure that we obtained a balanced perspective, we interviewed experts with a range of perspectives and from different types of organizations including government, academia, advocacy groups, and the private sector. For more information on our literature review and expert interviews, see appendix I. Some of the options have been proposed in various permutations. Our analysis is not intended to describe any one proposal. Rather, we describe the basic features of the option; these features may be common across proposals. GAO did not independently evaluate the efficacy of these options, nor by including them in this report are we providing a position on or endorsing any of these options.

Proposals to Expand the Use of Existing Tax Incentives to Save for Retirement

Some of the policy options we identified could expand the use of existing tax incentives for individuals to save for retirement during their working years (see table 3). These options could help lower- and moderate-income workers, as well as workers who take time out of the workforce to care for family members. Since women have lower earnings than men, on average, and are more likely to take time out of the workforce to care for family members, women may especially benefit from these options. However, pension experts are concerned that women may not be as financially literate as men, hindering them from taking full advantage of options for saving for retirement.[56]

Table 3: Proposals to Expand Use of Existing Tax Incentives to Save for Retirement

Policy option	Description of policy option	Potential effects on women
Automatic IRA	Employers who do not sponsor a pension plan would be required to automatically enroll employees in an IRA unless the employee opted out.[a] Automatic IRA proposals have been introduced before the four most recent Congresses.[b] However, this option would result in a loss of federal tax revenue.[c] Further, this kind of requirement could pose administrative burdens and costs for employers.	According to one study, lower- and moderate-income workers may be more likely to be eligible for automatic IRAs.[d] Women have lower incomes and retirement savings than men, but experts reported that automatic enrollment in IRAs could increase the number of women saving for retirement or increase their retirement savings. However, women from lower-income households may not be able to afford to make contributions to an IRA.
Expansion of Saver's Credit	The Saver's Credit—a tax credit for retirement savings for low- and middle-income workers—could be expanded in a number of ways. For example, some experts have called for making the credit refundable.[e] This option would result in a reduction in tax revenue.[f]	By enhancing the tax incentives to save for retirement, low- and middle-income workers may save more for retirement. However, women from lower-income households may choose not to take advantage of the credit because they may not be able to afford to contribute. Our previous work has shown that while the number of workers benefiting from an expansion of the Saver's Credit could be small, the increase in retirement savings could be sizable for those who do benefit.[g]

[56]We have previously reported that there is a need to improve individuals' financial literacy. Financial skills are increasingly important for ensuring a comfortable standard of living in retirement. GAO, *Financial Literacy: Enhancing the Effectiveness of the Federal Government's Role*, GAO-12-636T (Washington, D.C.: Apr. 26, 2012) and *Financial Literacy: Strengthening Partnerships in Challenging Times*, GAO-12-299SP (Washington, D.C.: Feb. 9, 2012).

Policy option	Description of policy option	Potential effects on women
Caregiver contributions to IRAs	Allow all caregivers to contribute to IRAs up to the qualified contribution limit, which would be based on the individual's adjusted gross income in the year prior to becoming a qualified caregiver. Currently, a married caregiver who has no compensation or whose compensation is less than her spouse, and who files a joint return, can contribute to an IRA by using her spouse's compensation in determining her maximum contributions to an IRA. If implemented, tax revenue could fall.	Women, who are more likely to take time out of the workforce to provide care for family members, could continue to save for retirement while providing care. However, women from lower-income households may not be able to afford to make contributions to an IRA while providing care to relatives.
Expand catch-up contributions	Currently, workers age 50 and over are permitted to make additional, annual "catch-up" tax-deferred contributions of up to $5,500 to their DC plans. Under this option, workers ages 40-49 would become eligible to make such contributions, and the contribution limits would be raised. Simultaneously, a campaign could be launched to promote the catch-up contribution option. By expanding tax incentives, however, more tax revenue could be deferred.	Women would be able to make larger contributions to DC plans for an additional decade, increasing their retirement savings. However, as we have previously reported, men are three times more likely than women to make catch-up contributions.[h] Because they have lower earnings than men, women may be constrained in their ability to save more. As a result, women may not choose to take advantage of extra years to make catch-up contributions.

Source: GAO analysis of literature and expert interviews.

[a]It has been proposed that certain types of firms, such as those with fewer than 10 employees, would be exempt from the automatic IRA requirement. Our prior work has analyzed the automatic IRA proposal. See GAO, *Retirement Savings: Automatic Enrollment Shows Promise for Some Workers, but Proposals to Broaden Retirement Savings for Other Workers Could Face Challenges*, GAO-10-31 (Washington, D.C.: Oct. 23, 2009) and *Private Pensions: Low Defined Contribution Plan Savings May Pose Challenges to Retirement Security, Especially for Many Low-Income Workers*, GAO-08-8 (Washington, D.C.: Nov. 29, 2007).

[b]See The Automatic IRA Act of 2012, H.R. 4049, 112th Cong. (2012) and the Automatic IRA Act of 2011, S. 1557, 112th Cong. (2011); the Automatic IRA Act of 2010, S. 3760 and H.R. 6099, 111th Cong. (2010); the Automatic IRA Act of 2007, S. 1141 and H.R. 2167, 110th Cong. (2007); and the Automatic IRA Act of 2006, S. 3952 and H.R. 6210, 109th Cong. (2006).

[c]Treasury has estimated that if automatic enrollment in IRAs and doubling an existing employer tax credit for starting an employer-sponsored pension plan were implemented by the end of calendar year 2013, then the revenue loss would be about $15 billion for fiscal years 2013-2022.

[d]Benjamin H. Harris and Ilana Fischer, *The Population of Workers Covered by the Auto IRA: Trends and Characteristics*, AARP Public Policy Institute (Washington, D.C.: Feb. 2012).

[e]Currently, the Saver's Credit is nonrefundable. A nonrefundable tax credit can reduce tax owed to zero, but it cannot be used to generate a refund payment to the filer in excess of taxes paid.

[f]The cost of expanding the Saver's Credit would depend on how the credit was expanded. For example, the President's fiscal year 2011 budget proposed expanding the Saver's Credit by making the credit refundable and providing a 50 percent match on retirement contributions of up to $1,000 for families earning $85,000 or less. The estimated cost of this expansion was $29.8 billion for fiscal years 2011–2020. See Office of Management and Budget, *Budget of the U.S. Government: Fiscal Year 2011* (Washington, D.C., Feb. 1, 2010).

[g]See GAO, *Private Pensions: Some Key Features Lead to an Uneven Distribution of Benefits*, GAO-11-333 (Washington, D.C.: Mar. 30, 2011).

[h]See GAO-11-333.

Proposals to Expand Opportunities to Accumulate Social Security Credits

Experts also identified a set of policy options that would offer new opportunities to accumulate earnings credits for Social Security (see table 4). These options could enhance the retirement security of workers who experience a period of unemployment or who take time out of the workforce to care for family members. For example, counting unemployment insurance payments as creditable earnings under Social Security may be particularly helpful for women who become unemployed later in life and experience a notable decrease in their assets and income. However, because they would extend eligibility or increase benefits, these options would increase costs for Social Security and decrease solvency.

Table 4: Proposals to Expand Eligibility and Opportunities to Accumulate Social Security Credits

Policy option	Description of policy option	Potential effects on women
Count unemployment insurance payments as creditable earnings under Social Security	Currently, workers do not receive earnings credits for unemployment compensation. However, two experts told us some countries consider unemployment compensation as creditable earnings under their social security systems. This allows workers to continue accruing earnings credits while unemployed. This option could increase costs and would decrease Social Security solvency.	According to two of the experts we spoke with, women who experience bouts of unemployment would receive more earnings credits under Social Security, potentially increasing their benefits. This option may also help women become eligible for benefits.
Allow care-giving credits for Social Security benefit calculations	Under the current system, Social Security eligibility and benefit amounts depend on the amount of time a worker spends in covered employment. Under this option, workers who take time out of the workforce to provide care could have their Social Security benefits adjusted. For example, the benefits formula could impute earnings for years with zero or low earnings due to care-giving.[a] In addition, this option would increase Social Security costs and decrease solvency.	Crediting time spent providing care could increase women's Social Security benefits or make them eligible for benefits. Our past work has shown that more women than men could benefit from care-giving credits.[b] However, as we have previously reported, care-giving credits may not reach the target population. For example, low-income people are less likely to be able to take time off from work. Therefore, people who have relatively higher incomes may benefit more from the creation of care-giving credits.[c]

Source: GAO analysis of literature and expert interviews.

[a]SSA's Office of the Chief Actuary has estimated the effect of providing a care-giving credit to parents with a child under 6 for up to 5 years. In 2011, the Office of the Chief Actuary estimated these proposals would decrease solvency by 0.24 percent of payroll. See http://www.ssa.gov/oact/solvency/provisions/index.html.

[b]See GAO-08-105.

[c]See GAO-10-101R.

Proposals to Expand Access to Retirement Savings and Strengthen Spousal Protections

Other policy options could either expand access to retirement savings in DC plans and IRAs or strengthen spousal protections for retirement savings (see table 5). These options could address a variety of challenges women face, including their lower levels of income in retirement. In addition, they could preserve retirement income after a divorce or after becoming widowed. For example, requiring that a wife provides consent whenever a husband takes a distribution from his DC savings would protect the wife's access to household income in retirement. However, these options could increase costs for plan sponsors. For example, requiring notarized spousal consent whenever a husband takes a distribution could increase the administrative costs that must be paid by plan sponsors.

Table 5: Proposals to Expand Access to Retirement Savings and Strengthen Spousal Protections

Policy option	Description of policy option	Potential effects on women
Lower DC plan eligibility requirements	Currently, employees are generally eligible for DC plans once they have at least 1,000 hours of service during a 12-month period. One proposal would require employers to offer DC plans to employees that have at least 500 hours of service per year for 3 years. This option could, in turn, increase costs for plan sponsors. It would also result in increased deferral of tax revenue if more workers made contributions to DC plans because DC contributions are typically tax-deferred.	Women, who tend to move in and out of the workforce and/or work part-time, could become eligible to participate in DC plans. If they choose to participate, their retirement savings would increase. However, over 75 percent of women covered by a pension are eligible to participate, so the number of women affected by this option may be limited. Further, part-time workers have lower earnings than full-time workers and may not be able to make contributions to DC plans.
Lower DC plan vesting requirements	Currently, ERISA requires that employees become vested in DC plans in no more than 3 or 6 years, depending on whether the plan calls for graded or cliff vesting, respectively.[a] Experts have called for lowering these vesting requirements. For example, one proposal calls for lowering vesting requirements to 2 years for plans with cliff vesting and 3 years for plans with graded vesting. Such options, however, could increase costs for plan sponsors and result in an increased deferral of tax revenue.	Women, who tend to move in and out of the workforce and/or work part-time, would become more likely to vest more of their employer-sponsored pension plans, improving their access to pension benefits and retirement savings. In our 2008 report on women's retirement income security, we simulated lowering vesting requirements. We found that women in the lowest income quintile saw the largest change in benefits. Similarly, never married and divorced women saw a bigger increase in benefits than did married and widowed women.[b]
Provide spousal protection provisions for DC savings	Currently, spousal consent is not required when married individuals take distributions from their IRA or DC savings. Under tax-qualified DB plans, the spouse must provide consent in order to elect a DB benefit that is not a qualified joint and survivor annuity. One proposal calls for requiring spousal consent for any distribution from an IRA or DC plan other than a joint and survivor annuity. This option could increase costs for plan sponsors and would defer tax revenue if requiring spousal consent results in individuals delaying withdrawals.	Spousal protections for DB and DC plans would be similar. These changes would help to ensure that women were involved with decisions that would affect their retirement income and, in turn, would help improve the adequacy of their retirement income. However, officials and experts have noted that spouses often give consent to select a DB benefit other than a joint and survivor annuity, raising questions about the effectiveness of placing the same spousal consent requirements on DC plans.

Source: GAO analysis of literature and expert interviews.

[a]ERISA, as amended, governs vesting periods. Plans with cliff vesting have a specified point at which participants have a right to all benefits accrued to date and benefits accrued thereafter. Plans with graded vesting give participants a right to an increasing percentage of their total accrued benefit over time. For more information, see GAO, *Answers to Key Questions about Private Pension Plans*, GAO-02-745SP (Washington, D.C.: Sept. 18, 2002).

[b]See GAO-08-105.

GAO-12-699 Women's Retirement Security

Proposals to Expand Opportunities for Saving Later in Life and Delay Social Security Benefit Receipt

Experts identified three policy options that could motivate women nearing retirement to remain in the workforce and delay claiming Social Security benefits, thereby giving them more time to save for retirement and increasing their Social Security benefits (see table 6). Because women tend to have less income in retirement than men, and because elderly women face higher poverty rates than elderly men, these options for boosting retirement savings and benefits may improve women's overall retirement income security. For example, the full retirement age for Social Security could be increased, thus providing workers who are able to work with an incentive to keep doing so—potentially saving more for retirement in the process. However, each of these options has disadvantages. In the case of increasing the full retirement age, this option may not prove to be effective because women may not be able to work longer or may choose to exit the workforce before the full retirement age. They would, in turn, suffer reductions in Social Security income.

Table 6: Proposals to Expand Opportunities for Saving Later in Life and Delay Social Security Benefit Receipt

Policy option	Description of policy option	Potential effects on women
Education on benefits of waiting to start collecting Social Security benefits	According to experts, many people do not realize that waiting to claim Social Security benefits can significantly increase monthly benefit amounts for the rest of their lives. Better educational outreach could increase awareness. If workers delay claiming Social Security benefits, income and payroll tax revenues would be increased and solvency would be improved. Employer pension costs could be increased if workers continue participating in their pension plans.	A larger monthly income could help many women avoid poverty in retirement and better protect against outliving their retirement assets. On the other hand, women may not have the savings they need or be able to keep working to have enough income to delay claiming.
Increase the early or full retirement ages	Experts told us the Social Security early or full retirement ages could be increased. By increasing the Social Security retirement ages, workers may choose to work longer, resulting in additional payroll tax revenue, which would improve solvency.[a] However, employer pension costs could be increased if workers continue participating in their pension plans.	Some experts told us that these changes could encourage people to delay retirement, potentially increasing their retirement savings. Others are concerned that these options would be harmful for women. For example, if the full retirement age is increased and women who planned to claim at the old full retirement age do not delay collecting Social Security benefits, they would receive a lower benefit.
Increase duration of unemployment benefits in lieu of applying for Social Security early	According to one expert we spoke with, the eligibility period for unemployment compensation could be extended further for older workers. This could increase federal tax revenue because unemployment compensation is taxable. However, paying more in unemployment benefits would exacerbate the financial challenges state unemployment insurance programs face.[b]	Unemployment can have a negative effect on women's income security. This option would provide additional income to unemployed older women, who may find it difficult to find another job. Instead of applying for early Social Security benefits, which results in a permanently lower benefit level, women could rely on unemployment compensation, thus preserving the value of their Social Security benefits.

Source: GAO analysis of literature and expert interviews.

Proposals to Ensure Lifetime Income

Experts also identified several policies that would ensure lifetime retirement income for women (see table 7). Women may especially benefit from these options, given that they (1) have lower levels of retirement income than men, (2) are more likely to live longer, and (3) are also more likely to become widowed. For example, Treasury recently proposed modifying the required minimum distribution rules so that individuals could use part of their retirement savings to purchase a longevity annuity.[57] This option would provide older women with guaranteed additional income, which may be helpful if they live long lives or outlive a spouse. These options, however, often have cost implications for either federal tax revenue or plan sponsors. For example, if individuals purchased longevity annuities using tax-qualified retirement savings, the tax revenue generated from withdrawing these savings would be deferred until the annuity started paying out.

---

[57]Certain provisions of the Internal Revenue Code set required minimum distributions from tax-deferred accounts, such as traditional IRAs and qualified plans, starting generally by April 1 in the year following the year in which the account holder reaches age 70 ½. These required minimum distributions help to ensure that account holders withdraw tax-deferred savings in retirement rather than accumulate savings for their estate.

Table 7: Proposals to Ensure Lifetime Income

Policy option	Description of policy option	Potential effects on women
Encourage DC plan sponsors to offer annuities as a distribution option for a portion or the entire DC account balance	Experts reported that steps could be taken to decrease the risks employers face when they offer an annuity as a distribution option for DC plans. For example, one expert told us the rules for using DC savings to purchase an annuity could be revised. These options could introduce greater costs and administrative burdens for plan sponsors.	More DC plan participants could have the opportunity to secure guaranteed lifetime income. This could be especially beneficial for women given that they tend to live longer than men, have higher poverty rates, and are more likely to be widowed.
Modify required minimum distribution rules to allow for longevity annuities	This option would modify the required minimum distribution rules so that it is easier to purchase longevity annuities with a portion of DC plan assets.[a] In February, Treasury proposed a regulation that would alter the required minimum distribution rules to make it easier for individuals to use a portion of their savings to purchase longevity annuities.[b] Tax revenue would be deferred until the annuity starts paying out.	A longevity annuity would decrease the chances that a woman would outlive her retirement savings. Given women's tendency to live longer than men, as well as their higher poverty rates and likelihood of being widowed, this option could be especially beneficial for improving women's retirement income security.
Reduce eligibility requirements for divorced spousal benefits under Social Security	Currently, a divorced spouse can receive benefits based on a retired worker's earnings record if the marriage lasted at least 10 years, and the spouse is unmarried and at least 62 years old. Experts have recommended expanding eligibility for divorce benefits to require a minimum of 7 years of marriage. Additionally, some experts have suggested marriage years could also be accumulated across multiple marriages. This option would increase Social Security costs and the administrative burden for SSA, while decreasing solvency.	More divorced women would qualify for spousal benefits. One study estimated that lowering the marriage-duration requirement from 10 to 7 years would increase benefits for about 8 percent of all divorced women age 62 and over in the year 2030.[c] However, as we have previously reported, this option could benefit higher-income women who are not economically vulnerable and it would not benefit women who were never married.[d]

Source: GAO analysis of literature and expert interviews.

[a]A longevity annuity (sometimes referred to as "longevity insurance" or a "deeply deferred annuity") is an income stream that can be purchased at or near retirement but begins at an advanced age—for example, age 85—and continues as long as the individual lives.

[b]Longevity Annuity Contracts, 77 Fed. Reg. 5443 (Feb. 3, 2012).

[c]Christopher R. Tamborini and Kevin Whitman, "Lowering Social Security's Duration-of-Marriage Requirement: Distributional Effects for Future Female Retirees," *Journal of Women and Aging* vol. 22 (2010).

[d]GAO, *Social Security: Options to Protect Benefits for Vulnerable Groups When Addressing Program Solvency*, GAO-10-101R (Washington, D.C.: Dec. 7, 2009).

Proposals to Ensure Income Adequacy

There are also a number of policy options that could enhance Social Security benefits for vulnerable groups at risk of not having sufficient income or assets in retirement, including widows, divorced women, low-income women and women age 85 and over (see table 8).[58] For example, increasing the Social Security Survivor's benefit to 75 percent of the deceased worker's benefit would provide widows with more monthly income, helping to keep some women out of poverty. However, all of these options would increase existing costs or introduce new costs and, in turn, would decrease the solvency of the system.

Table 8: Proposals to Ensure Income Adequacy

Policy option	Description of policy option	Potential effects on women
Use consumer price index for the elderly (CPI-E) to calculate Social Security cost-of-living adjustments	Currently, the Consumer Price Index for Urban Wage Earners and Clerical Workers (CPI-W) is used to calculate annual cost-of-living adjustments for Social Security benefits. However, some experts argue that the CPI-W does not accurately reflect expenses for the elderly. The CPI-E, an index designed to represent expenses of those age 62 and over,[a] could be used to calculate cost-of-living adjustments for Social Security recipients. Experts say an advantage of the CPI-E is that it more accurately reflects the typically larger share of expenditures older Americans spend on medical care. This option would decrease Social Security solvency because it would generally increase benefit levels and, therefore, costs.[b]	Advocates for the CPI-E reported that it more accurately reflect expenses for retirees, thereby improving income adequacy by providing more appropriate cost-of-living adjustments. While all Social Security recipients would benefit, women could benefit more than men as they tend to live longer. Moreover, benefit increases compound over time. However, some advocates believe benefits would still be insufficient under the CPI-E.
Update the Social Security Special Minimum Benefit	Currently, Social Security includes a Special Primary Insurance Amount (also referred to as the Special Minimum Benefit) that is intended to reduce poverty among retired lifetime low-wage workers. However, very few people receive this benefit.[c] There are several options for increasing the minimum benefit. For example, one proposal would increase the minimum benefit and index it to wages.[d] While benefits would increase, decreasing poverty for some beneficiaries, this option would increase costs and decrease solvency.	An increased Special Minimum Benefit could keep more elderly women out of poverty by increasing their monthly income. In addition, our past work found that while the share of women affected by the minimum benefit was fairly similar across marital statuses (never-married, divorced, married and widowed), never-married and divorced women had much larger percent changes in median benefits.[e]
Provide an additional Social Security benefit to the oldest old	Social Security recipients over the age of 80 or 85 could receive an additional benefit, such as an extra 5 percent on top of their regular benefit. While this option would increase benefits for the oldest old, it would also increase costs and decrease solvency.[f]	Women, who tend to live longer than men, would be more likely to receive this extra benefit. Older women may need extra benefit as income and assets may have been used to care for a deceased spouse or to pay for increasing medical costs. An additional benefit may be particularly helpful for low-income women.

[58]Experts we spoke with also identified women without long-term care insurance as a vulnerable population. Although the lack of long-term care insurance does put women at risk of income insecurity, in general, we did not identify any long-term care policy options that addressed retirement income specifically.

Policy option	Description of policy option	Potential effects on women
Increase Social Security Survivor's benefits to 75%	Currently, when someone is widowed, total household income from Social Security decreases by one-third if the couple's benefits had been based on one spouse's work history and up to 50 percent if both spouses had been receiving retired worker benefits. Survivor's benefits could be increased to 75 percent of the couple's retired-workers benefits. Experts have proposed calculating this new benefit in different ways. For example, the surviving spouse could receive 75 percent of the couple's retired-workers benefit but the benefit would be capped at the maximum earner's benefit or at the benefit of the "lifelong average earner." However, increasing benefits would increase costs and decrease solvency.	Increasing Survivor's benefits would increase income for widowed women. Widowhood can have a devastating effect on women's household assets and income. Further, women are more likely than men to be widowed so they would be more likely to benefit from an increase in the survivor's benefit. In fact, when we simulated the effects of this option in 2007, we found that three times the number of women as men were affected. However, the magnitude of the benefit increase was larger for men than for women.[g]
Increase Social Security spousal benefits for divorced spouses	Currently, divorced spouses who qualify for spousal benefits receive a benefit equal up to 50 percent of the worker's benefits. This option would raise benefits for divorced spouses to 75 percent of the former spouse's benefit while the former spouse is still alive. Upon the death of the former spouse, the divorced spouse would receive the full widow's benefit of 100 percent. This benefit increase would decrease solvency because it would increase costs.	Divorce can result in a substantial loss of assets and income for women. Some experts argue that a 50 percent benefit is not enough to keep divorced women from falling into poverty. It has been estimated that increasing the benefit rate for divorced spouses to 75 percent would lower the poverty rate among divorced spouses from 30 percent to 11 percent.[h]
Increase Social Security benefits for disabled surviving spouses	Currently, to qualify for disabled surviving spouse benefits, disabled surviving spouses must be at least age 50 and have become disabled before or within 7 years of the spouse's death or before or within 7 years after last being eligible for benefits as a caretaking parent or eligible surviving child. In addition, disabled surviving spouses younger than the full retirement age generally receive lower benefits than those who wait to receive their benefits until the full retirement age. This option would raise benefits for disabled surviving spouses to 100 percent of the deceased spouse's benefit. It would also remove the 7 year limitation and the age 50 requirement. Lastly, it would make divorced spouses who are disabled eligible for benefits on the same basis as disabled surviving spouses. Although benefits would increase, Social Security solvency would decrease.	Both divorce and widowhood can result in a decrease in retirement security. Further, disabled surviving spouses, including those who have been divorced, cannot work and may have no partner to depend on for support. In addition, disability issues affect a surprisingly high number of divorced spouses, making them more vulnerable to income insecurity. One study estimated that more than one-fifth of all divorced spouses had health problems that meet disability criteria established by SSA.[i]
Increase continuation percentage for qualified joint-and-survivor annuities	Currently, if a worker receives a joint and survivor annuity, when the worker passes away, the spouse continues to receive the annuity, but at not less than 50 percent of the amount the worker received. This option would increase the minimum continuation percentage to 66 or 75 percent.	It is about 40 percent more expensive to live as a single retiree than as a married retiree. After becoming widowed, household annuity income would be reduced by a smaller amount than it is currently. However, by increasing the continuation percentage, the cost of the joint-and-survivor annuity could increase.

Source: GAO analysis of literature and expert interviews.

[a]The CPI-E is an experimental index developed by the Bureau of Labor Statistics. It takes into account increased utilization of medical care by the elderly. Officials from the Bureau of Labor Statistics have cautioned against using the CPI-E for pension and other adjustments because it is only an approximation of an index for older Americans. See GAO, *Income Security: Older Adults and the 2007-2009 Recession*. GAO-12-76 (Washington, D.C.: Oct. 17, 2011).

[b]SSA's Office of the Chief Actuary has estimated the effect of using the CPI-E to calculate cost-of-living-adjustments would have on solvency. In 2011, the Office of the Chief Actuary estimated that solvency would be decreased by 0.35 percent of payroll. See
http://www.ssa.gov/oact/solvency/provisions/index.html.

[c]Currently, few people qualify for the special minimum benefit because the eligibility threshold has not kept pace with wage growth.

[d]SSA's Office of the Chief Actuary has estimated the effects various proposals to increase the Special Minimum Benefit would have on solvency. In 2011, the Office of the Chief Actuary estimated these proposals would decrease solvency by 0.10 to 0.28 percent of payroll. For these estimates, see
http://www.ssa.gov/oact/solvency/provisions/index.html.

[e]See GAO-08-105.

[f]SSA's Office of the Chief Actuary has estimated the effects various proposals to increase benefits for those age 85 and over would have on solvency. In 2011, the Office of the Chief Actuary estimated these proposals would decrease solvency by 0.10 to 0.13 percent of payroll. For these estimates, see
http://www.ssa.gov/oact/solvency/provisions/index.html.

[g]See GAO-08-105.

[h]Alison M. Shelton and Dawn Nuschler, *Social Security: Revisiting Benefits for Spouses and Survivors*, Congressional Research Service (Washington, D.C.: Nov. 5, 2010).

[i]David A. Weaver, "The Economic Well-Being of Social Security Beneficiaries, with an Emphasis on Divorced Beneficiaries," *Social Security Bulletin*, vol. 60, no. 4 (1997).

Concluding Observations

To retirement security experts, our findings paint a familiar if disconcerting picture. Although increases in women's labor force and retirement plan participation have led to a marginal improvement in women's prospects for achieving a more secure retirement, our report also highlights the substantial risks women continue to face in accumulating adequate retirement income. Yet, despite the differential risks women face, retirement security in America continues to be a national dilemma that transcends gender differences. It is important to note that much of the relative improvement in women's retirement security has been a consequence of deterioration in men's retirement security. Recent economic volatility, coupled with the continued shift toward defined contribution plans, exposes all workers to more financial risk than previous generations. Further, older workers' financial security is increasingly dependent on individual choices regarding how much to save, how to invest those savings, at what age to retire, and how to make those savings last throughout retirement. Much of the total workforce continues to approach retirement age with no traditional pension. Unchecked, this problem will only grow in severity.

Nevertheless, women face a unique set of circumstances, which warrant special attention. In particular, our findings show that the disruptions that occur as a result of later-in-life events, such as divorce and widowhood, can be financially devastating for women. In addition, women's greater likelihood of being single, higher life expectancy, and lower average earnings continue to make saving for retirement and avoiding late-life poverty a challenge.

The challenges facing women's retirement income security do not lack for potential resolutions. In fact, our discussions with experts identified a number of policy options that would improve retirement income security for women. These options range from changes to Social Security to altering the private pension system. While these options involve tradeoffs and difficult choices, they have the potential to improve the retirement income security of men as well. Ultimately, such efforts provide opportunities to improve the retirement security of many Americans.

Agency Comments

We provided a draft of this report to the Department of Labor, the Department of the Treasury, and the Social Security Administration for review and comment. While none of the agencies provided official comments, each provided technical comments, which we incorporated as appropriate.

As agreed with your office, unless you publicly announce its contents earlier, we plan no further distribution until 30 days after the date of this letter. At that time, we will send copies of this report to the Secretary of Labor, the Secretary of the Treasury, the Commissioner of Social Security, and other interested parties. In addition, the report will be available at no charge on the GAO website at http://www.gao.gov.

If you or your staff have any questions about this report, please contact me at (202) 512-7215 or jeszeckc@gao.gov. Contact points for our Offices of Congressional Relations and Public Affairs may be found on the last page of this report. GAO staff who made contributions to this report are listed in appendix II.

Sincerely yours,

Charles A. Jeszeck
Director
Education, Workforce,
    and Income Security

Appendix I: Objective, Scope, and Methods

To analyze factors that affect women's retirement security, we examined (1) how women's access to and participation in employer-sponsored retirement plans compare to men's and how they have changed over time; (2) how women's retirement income compares to men's and how the composition of their income has changed with economic conditions and trends in pension design; (3) how events occurring later in life affect women's retirement income; and (4) what policy options are available to help increase women's retirement income security. This appendix provides a detailed account of the information and methods we used to answer these questions. Section 1 describes the key information sources we used. Sections 2 through 4 describe the empirical methods we used to answer questions 1 through 3 respectively and the results of supplementary analyses.

Section 1: Information Sources

To answer our questions, we obtained information from a variety of sources including two nationally representative surveys—the Survey of Income and Program Participation (SIPP) and the Health and Retirement Study (HRS)—the academic literature on retirement security, and a range of experts in the area of women's retirement security. Table 9 summarizes the data sources used to answer each question. This section provides a description of our data sources and the steps we took to ensure their reliability.

Table 9: Data Sources Used for Each Reporting Objective

	SIPP data	HRS data	Academic literature	Expert opinions[a]
Objective 1: Women and men's access to employer-sponsored pension plans	X		X	X
Objective 2: Women's and men's retirement income sources	X		X	X
Objective 3: Impact of late-in-life events on retirement income and assets		X	X	X
Objective 4: Policy options			X	X

Source: GAO.

[a]Expert opinions were gathered from the literature and our interviews. We interviewed experts from government, academia, advocacy groups, and the private sector. For more information about our literature review and expert interviews, see below.

Survey of Income and Program Participation

To answer Questions 1 and 2, we analyzed data collected through the SIPP, a nationally representative survey conducted by the U.S. Census Bureau that collects detailed information on income sources and pension plan coverage, among many other areas. The survey is conducted in a series of national panels, with sample sizes ranging from approximately 14,000 to 36,700 interviewed households. The duration of each panel ranges from 2 ½ years to 4 years. Within each panel, the data are collected in a series of "waves" which take place in 4-month cycles. Within each wave, Census administers a core survey consisting of questions that are asked at every interview, and several modules relating to a particular topic. We used data from the core survey and the topical module on retirement and pension coverage from the last four SIPP panels, which began in 1996, 2001, 2004, and 2008 respectively. For all but the 2008 panel, the topical module on retirement and pension coverage was administered in Wave 7. For objective 1, we matched core data from Wave 3 of the 2008 panel with the topical module data, which was also administered in Wave 3. This ensured that the demographic data used in the analysis for that objective would match the time frame of the topical module data. However, to obtain the most up to date income data for objective 2, we used core data from Wave 7, which was the most recently available data as of October 2011. Table 10 shows the waves and questionnaires we used to answer each objective. It also shows the years that the data were collected during each panel and wave listed. The bolded years correspond to the years of data that are presented in the figures in objectives 1 and 2.

Table 10: SIPP Panels, Waves, and Questionnaires Used to Answer Objective 1 and Objective 2

	Year data were collected	Objective 1	Objective 2
1996 Panel, Wave 7, Core questionnaire	1997, 1998[a]	X	X
1996 Panel, Wave 7, Topical Module on Retirement and Pension Plan Coverage	1997, 1998[a]	X	
2001 Panel, Wave 7, Core questionnaire	2002, 2003[a]	X	X
2001 Panel, Wave 7, Topical Module on Retirement and Pension Plan Coverage	2002, 2003[a]	X	
2004 Panel, Wave 7, Core questionnaire	2005, 2006[a]	X	X

	Year data were collected	Objective 1	Objective 2
2004 Panel, Wave 7, Topical Module on Retirement and Pension Plan Coverage	2005, 2006[a]	X	
2008 Panel, Wave 3, Core questionnaire	2009	X	X
2008 Panel, Wave 3, Topical Module on Retirement and Pension Plan Coverage	2009	X	
2008 Panel, Wave 7, Core questionnaire	2010		X

Source: GAO.

[a]In this report, the data are described by referring to the year from which the majority of the data was collected. For example, the 2001 Wave 7 data is descr bed as "2003 data" because the reference periods for 10 of the 16 rotation groups in this wave were in calendar year 2003.

In comparison to other nationally representative surveys, the SIPP had several main advantages. First, the SIPP collects separate information on defined benefit (DB) and defined contribution (DC) plans. Other surveys, such as the Current Population Survey, do not distinguish between income from and participation in DB and DC plans. Second, the SIPP sample is larger than comparable surveys, such as the Survey of Consumer Finances (SCF). Consequently, it is possible to produce point estimates for demographic subcategories with a higher degree of reliability. Further, in comparison to the SCF, which oversamples wealthy households, the SIPP oversamples lower-income households—arguably an important component of an analysis of income security.

Despite its advantages, the SIPP has two limitations for our analysis. First, as with most survey data, SIPP data are self-reported. This can be problematic for the reporting of data on income sources and pension plan participation. For example, respondents might incorrectly report that they participate in a pension plan when they do not participate in one.[1] Second, despite the fact that SIPP differentiates between participation in

---

[1]For more information regarding such misreporting, see Irena Dushi, Howard M. Iams, and Jules Lichtenstein, "Assessment of Retirement Plan Coverage by Firm Size, Using W-2 Tax Records," *Social Security Bulletin*, vol. 71, no. 2 (2011).

a DB or DC plan, it does not contain full information on whether an individual's employer offers a DB plan.[2]

Health and Retirement Study

To answer question 3—on the effects of events occurring later in life on women's retirement income security—we analyzed data collected through the HRS, a nationally representative survey primarily sponsored by the National Institute of Aging and conducted by the Institute for Social Research at the University of Michigan. This longitudinal survey collects data on individuals over age 50 and contains detailed information on health, marital status, assets, income, and care for elders. Respondents were first surveyed in 1992, when they were age 51 to 61 and continued to be surveyed every 2 years. Additional cohorts were added in later years to maintain the representation of the older population. Table 11 presents the cohorts that are included in the HRS sample. Respondents are resurveyed every 2 years. The data in our analysis span from the initial 1992 survey through the early release data for 2010, the most current data available. Our analysis follows over 30,000 individuals from the HRS sample.

Table 11: Birth Years for the HRS Cohorts and the Year Data Collection Began for Each Cohort

Cohort	Birth years	Year data collection began
AHEAD[a]	1923 and earlier	1993
Children of the Depression Era (CODA)[a]	1924-1930	1998
Original HRS cohort	1931-1941	1992
War Babies[a]	1942-1947	1998
Early Baby Boomers	1948-1953	2004

Source: RAND HRS Data Documentation, Version L.

[a]The Asset and Health Dynamics of the Oldest Old (AHEAD) survey began collecting data in 1993. Originally, the HRS and AHEAD were separate but related surveys. The AHEAD survey was initially funded as a supplement to the HRS. In 1998, the two surveys merged and the CODA and War Babies cohorts were added to the survey.

---

[2]The survey contains catch-all questions for whether an individual's employer offers a DC plan, but it does not contain similar questions for DB plans. Specifically, those who are not included in their employer's plan are not asked whether their employer offers a DB plan.

One of the main advantages of the HRS is that the same households are interviewed at different points of time, allowing us to examine the correlation of changes in life events to changes in household assets and income. Further, RAND, a research organization, cleans and processes the HRS data to create a user-friendly longitudinal dataset that has consistent and intuitive naming conventions, model-based imputations for missing wealth and income data, and spousal counterparts of most individual-level variables. We used these data for our analysis.

However, there are three limitations for our analysis. First, the women currently in the HRS survey may have very different retirement experiences from women in the workforce today due to changes in demographic trends and workforce participation. Second, as with the SIPP, data from the HRS are self-reported. Third, total household assets cannot be broken out at the individual level.

Data Reliability

For each of the datasets described above, we conducted a data reliability assessment of selected variables by conducting electronic data tests for completeness and accuracy, reviewing documentation on the dataset, or interviewing knowledgeable officials about how the data are collected and maintained and their appropriate uses. When we learned that particular fields were not sufficiently reliable, we did not use them in our analysis. For example, we chose not to use data from the SIPP Topical Module on Annual Income and Retirement Accounts because many of the fields in that survey are not edited by the Census Bureau. For the purposes of our analysis, we found the variables that we ultimately reported on to be sufficiently reliable.

Literature Review and Interviews

To gain an understanding of the challenges women face in attaining a secure retirement and policy options that could enhance women's retirement security, we conducted an extensive literature review and interviewed a range of experts. To identify existing studies, we conducted searches of various databases, such as EconLit, Electronic Collections Online, ProQuest, Academic OneFile, WorldCat, and Policy File. From these sources, we identified 128 articles that appeared in journals since 2007 and were relevant to our research objective on policy options that could enhance women's retirement security. From the articles identified in the preliminary search, we reviewed article abstracts, when available, to determine which articles contained information germane to our report and reviewed those articles. In addition, we reviewed articles that were collected during the previous GAO study on women's retirement security that contained information relevant to our empirical analyses, described below, and reviewed articles that were suggested to us by the experts we interviewed. We performed these searches and identified articles from May 2011 to October 2011.

To supplement the literature review, we conducted interviews with experts. To ensure that we obtained a balanced perspective, we interviewed experts with a range of perspectives and from different types of organizations including government, academia, advocacy groups, and the private sector. We also consulted several experts in government and academia on technical issues related to our analysis. Specifically, we interviewed agency officials at the departments of the Treasury and Labor, the Social Security Administration, and the Bureau of the Census; academic experts at the Employee Benefits Research Institute, Heritage Foundation, University of Pennsylvania, Stanford University, Urban Institute, and Wellesley College; and industry experts and advocates from the American Council on Life Insurers, Anna Rappaport Consulting, Financial Engines, the Institute for Women's Policy Research, the National Women's Law Center, AARP, the Pension Rights Center, the National Academy of Social Insurance, Social Security Works, and the Women's Institute for a Secure Retirement.

Section 2: Methods for Comparing Working Women's and Men's Access to and Participation in Employer-Sponsored Pension Plans

To determine the proportion of men and women that (1) work for an employer that offers a plan, (2) are eligible for a plan, and (3) participate in a plan, we used data from the SIPP topical module on retirement and pension plan coverage. Specifically, we constructed five dummy variables using a combination of various questions in the SIPP. Table 12 shows the information we used to construct each variable. For each of these variables, we used SIPP individual-level weights to compute point estimates and, in conjunction with other factors, calculate the standard errors of those estimates so that we could accurately account for the complex survey design. We consulted statisticians from the U.S. Bureau of the Census on the appropriate use of these weights.

Table 12: Information Used from SIPP to Construct Key Variables

Variable	Constructed with:
Worker has employer that offers either a DB or a DC pension plan to some employees	A combination of two questions. One question asks whether the individual's job or business has any kind of pension or retirement plan for anyone in the company or organization, and a subsequent clarifying question asks if the individual's job or business offers a DC plan.
Worker has employer that offers a DC pension plan to some employees	A combination of questions. If the respondent replied yes to the question listed above, a follow-up question is asked about whether the respondent participates in the plan, and if so, the type of plan. This series of questions enables us to identify, among those who participate, whether the individual's employer offers a DC plan. For those that said that their employer does not offer a pension or retirement plan, and those who said that their employer offers a plan but it does not include a DC-type component, SIPP asks a follow-up question about whether the employer offers a DC-type plan. By combining these two sets of information, we were able to construct a dummy variable to indicate whether the individual's employer offers a DC plan.
Worker is eligible for employer-sponsored plan	A question in the SIPP topical module on retirement and pension plan coverage that asks the reason for not participating in the employer's plan. We defined individuals as not eligible if they listed one of the following reasons for not participating: no one in their type of job is eligible; they don't work enough hours, days, weeks or months; they don't have enough tenure in the job; they are too young; they started their job too close to retirement. We defined individuals as eligible if they participated in the plan or listed some other reason for not participating.
Worker participates in employer-sponsored DB or DC plan	A combination of two questions. One question asks whether the individual participates in the employer-sponsored plan, and a subsequent clarifying question asks if the individual participates in an employer-sponsored DC plan.
Worker participates in employer-sponsored DC plan	A combination of questions. If the respondent replied yes to the question above and the respondent indicates that the type of plan in which he or she participated was a DC plan.

Source: GAO analysis of SIPP questionnaire.

To better understand the factors that might explain gender differences in each of these variables, we developed a series of empirical models. Following the literature, we controlled for the following factors in our models: (1) demographic characteristics including gender, age, marital status, children present in the household, single parenthood, race and ethnicity, citizenship, immigrant status, and education level; and (2) occupational characteristics including part-time employment status, self-employment status, years of tenure, work experience, occupation, industry, sector, union status, and size of employing firm.[3] To estimate these models, we used logistic regression—an appropriate technique when the dependent variable is binary, or has two categories such as participating in a plan or not participating in a plan. Logistic regression also allows for the coefficients to be converted into odds ratios, which are described below.

We conducted the modeling analyses in a series of steps whereby with each step, the sample of men and women that was included in the analysis was conditional on the previous step. Specifically, the first analysis involved analyzing the probability of working for an employer that offered a pension plan for all workers in the sample. The second analysis involved analyzing the probability of being eligible for a plan for those men and women that worked for an employer offering a plan. The third analysis involved analyzing the probability of participating in a plan for those that were eligible for their employer-sponsored plan.

Changes in the Working Population Over Time by Gender

In conjunction with understanding the factors associated with each dependent variable in our models, it is essential to also understand how women and men differ in those factors. Taken together, the information from the model and information from a comparison of men's and women's characteristics enables us to understand what factors make women more or less likely to be employed by an employer that offers a plan, be eligible for the plan, and participate in the plan. For example, if we know that women are disproportionately more likely to work part-time and that part-time status is an important factor associated with plan participation, we can infer that women's higher rates of part-time status might contribute to their lower rates of plan participation. Table 13 compares the characteristics of men and women for each of the factors that we control for, across each year of the study period.

---

[3]Note that in the models we present, we did not include income as a control variable. Income can be considered to be endogenously (or simultaneously) determined with an individual's decision to work for a particular employer that might be offering a plan and therefore have the potential to bias the model estimates. For example, one might deliberately choose to work in a lower-paid government position to ensure access to a DB plan. We did run versions of our model with income included as a control and found that it was significantly associated with the likelihood of working for an employer that offers a plan and of participating in a plan.

Generally, the characteristics of men and women in the working population did not change dramatically over the study period. Correspondingly, when we compare men and women in each year, several relationships between them were consistent across all of the study years. In terms of demographic characteristics, women were more likely than men to be widowed and divorced. Women were also more likely to have children present in the household, be single parents, and work part time. A higher proportion of men than women were Hispanic, and this proportion increased over the study period.[4]

In terms of occupational characteristics, several gender differences persisted across the study years. Women consistently had higher levels of education and were more likely to work in the public or nonprofit sectors. Men were more likely to work in the private sector, be self-employed, have longer tenure at their current position, have more work experience, and to be in a union.

Although the occupational and industry categories in the SIPP data changed midway through the study periods, the distributions of men and women across occupations and industry were generally consistent for the last 2 study years. Specifically, the top three occupations for women were office and administrative support; sales and related services; and education, training, and library services, with 20, 10, and 10 percent of women working in these occupations respectively in 2009. Men tended not to be as concentrated in just a few occupations. In 2009, the highest proportions of men were employed in management (9 percent), sales and related occupations (8 percent), construction and extraction (8 percent), and transportation and material moving (8 percent). Similarly, in 2009, the top three industries for women were health care and social assistance (21 percent), educational services (14 percent), and retail trade (10 percent). For men in this year, the top three industries in which men were employed were manufacturing (13 percent), construction (9 percent), and retail trade (9 percent).

---

[4]This result is consistent with Census findings, which note a higher male-to-female ratio among the Hispanic population in the United States than among the general population.

Table 13: Characteristics of the Working Population over Time

| | 1999 | | 2003 | | 2006 | | 2009 | |
| | Percentage of | | Percentage of | | Percentage of | | Percentage of | |
	Men	Women	Men	Women	Men	Women	Men	Women
Gender	53	47	53	47	53	47	53	47
Age groups								
18-24	12	13	12	13	13	13	12	13
25-34	26	25	24	23	23	22	23	22
35-44	29	29	27	27	26	25	24	23
45-54	22	22	24	25	24	25	25	26
55-64	11	11	13	13	14	14	16	16
Marital status								
Married	62	57	61	57	59	56	59	55
Widowed	1	3	1	2	1	2	1	2
Divorced	9	13	10	14	10	13	9	13
Separated	2	3	2	3	2	2	2	2
Never married	26	23	27	24	29	26	29	27
Children in the household	46	49	44	46	44	47	42	44
Single parent	8	16	7	16	8	16	8	16
Race and ethnicity								
White, Non-Hispanic	76	75	73	72	69	70	69	70
Black, Non-Hispanic	9	12	9	12	10	12	9	12
Hispanic	11	9	14	11	15	11	16	12
Asian, Non-Hispanic	3	4	4	4	4	3	4	4
Other, Non-Hispanic	1	1	1	1	2	3	2	3
Citizenship								
Noncitizen	7	6	9	6	10	7	10	6
Immigrant status								
Naturalized immigrant	4	4	5	5	6	6	7	7
Education level								
No high school diploma	12	9	12	8	8	5	8	5

	1999 Percentage of		2003 Percentage of		2006 Percentage of		2009 Percentage of	
	Men	Women	Men	Women	Men	Women	Men	Women
High school diploma	32	30	29	27	30	26	27	23
Some college	30	34	30	35	35	39	35	39
Bachelor's degree or higher	26	27	29	29	28	31	30	33
Part-time status[a]								
Part time	22	37	23	38	22	36	26	37
Self-employment status								
Self-employed	16	10	15	10	15	10	16	10
Average years of tenure at current job	8.0	6.9	8.0	7.0	7.8	7.2	8.2	7.7
Work experience								
Less than 5 years	26	29	26	31	25	28	26	30
5 to 9 years	14	17	14	15	14	16	14	16
10 to 15 years	11	12	11	11	10	11	12	12
More than 15 years	49	43	49	43	50	45	48	41
Average years of total work experience	10.8	9.4	11.1	9.7	11.4	10.3	11.9	10.7
Sector								
Private for profit	70	63	69	62	71	62	68	61
Private not for profit	4	10	4	10	4	10	4	10
Government	13	18	13	19	12	18	14	19
Family worker without pay	1	1	0	1	0	1	0	1
Not in universe	13	7	13	8	12	8	13	8
Union status								
In union	17	12	15	12	14	12	15	13
Occupation								
Management	NA	NA	NA	NA	9	7	9	7
Business and Financial Operations	NA	NA	NA	NA	3	4	3	5
Computer and Mathematical	NA	NA	NA	NA	3	2	4	1
Architecture and Engineering	NA	NA	NA	NA	3	1	3	1
Life, Physical, and Social Services	NA	NA	NA	NA	1	1	1	1
Community and Social Services	NA	NA	NA	NA	1	2	1	2

GAO-12-699 Women's Retirement Security

	1999		2003		2006		2009	
	Percentage of		Percentage of		Percentage of		Percentage of	
	Men	Women	Men	Women	Men	Women	Men	Women
Legal	NA	NA	NA	NA	1	1	1	1
Education, Training, and Library	NA	NA	NA	NA	3	10	3	10
Arts, Design, Entertainment, Sports, and Media	NA	NA	NA	NA	1	1	1	1
Healthcare Practitioners and Technical	NA	NA	NA	NA	2	8	2	8
Healthcare Support	NA	NA	NA	NA	0	4	0	4
Protective Service	NA	NA	NA	NA	3	1	3	1
Food Preparation and Serving Related	NA	NA	NA	NA	4	6	4	6
Building and Grounds Cleaning and Maintenance	NA	NA	NA	NA	4	3	4	3
Personal Care and Service	NA	NA	NA	NA	1	4	1	4
Sales and Related	NA	NA	NA	NA	8	10	8	10
Office and Administrative Support	NA	NA	NA	NA	7	22	6	20
Farming, Forestry, and Fishing	NA	NA	NA	NA	1	0	1	0
Construction and Extraction	NA	NA	NA	NA	9	0	8	0
Installation, Repair, and Maintenance	NA	NA	NA	NA	6	0	6	0
Production	NA	NA	NA	NA	9	4	7	3
Transportation and Material Moving	NA	NA	NA	NA	9	2	8	2
Not in universe[b]	NA	NA	NA	NA	12	7	14	8
Industry								
Agriculture	NA	NA	NA	NA	1	0	1	1
Mining	NA	NA	NA	NA	1	0	1	0
Utilities	NA	NA	NA	NA	1	0	1	0
Construction	NA	NA	NA	NA	10	1	9	1
Manufacturing	NA	NA	NA	NA	15	7	13	6
Wholesale Trade	NA	NA	NA	NA	4	2	3	2
Retail Trade	NA	NA	NA	NA	10	10	9	10
Transportation and Warehousing	NA	NA	NA	NA	5	2	5	2
Information	NA	NA	NA	NA	2	2	2	2
Finance and Insurance	NA	NA	NA	NA	3	6	3	6

GAO-12-699 Women's Retirement Security

Appendix I: Objective, Scope, and Methods

	1999		2003		2006		2009	
	Percentage of		Percentage of		Percentage of		Percentage of	
	Men	Women	Men	Women	Men	Women	Men	Women
Real Estate and Rental and Leasing	NA	NA	NA	NA	1	2	1	1
Professional, Scientific, and Technical	NA	NA	NA	NA	5	5	5	5
Management, Administrative and Support	NA	NA	NA	NA	4	3	4	3
Educational Services	NA	NA	NA	NA	5	14	6	14
Health Care and Social Assistance	NA	NA	NA	NA	4	19	4	21
Arts, Entertainment, and Recreation	NA	NA	NA	NA	1	2	2	2
Accommodations and Food Services	NA	NA	NA	NA	5	7	6	8
Other Services (Except Public Administration)	NA	NA	NA	NA	3	4	3	4
Public Administration	NA	NA	NA	NA	6	5	5	5
Active duty	NA	NA	NA	NA	1	0	1	0
Not in universe[b]	NA	NA	NA	NA	12	7	13	8
Household income bracket								
Less than $20,000	7	8	6	8	7	8	8	9
$20,000-$40,000	17	18	16	18	16	17	16	16
$40,000-$60,000	20	20	19	19	19	19	18	19
$60,000-$80,000	18	17	17	17	16	16	16	15
Greater than $80,000	38	36	41	39	42	41	41	40
Firm size								
Under 25 employees	18	19	18	19	19	19	18	18
25 to 100 employees	12	11	12	11	11	11	11	11
100+ employees	58	62	58	62	57	63	58	63
Not in universe[b]	13	7	13	8	12	8	13	8

Source: GAO analysis of SIPP data.

Note: The categories for occupation and industry changed between the 2001 and 2003 SIPP panels. We present the categories for the two most recent panels.

[a]Part-time status is defined as working 35 hours or less per week during the reference period.

[b]The category "Not in universe" includes self-employed individuals.

GAO-12-699 Women's Retirement Security

Factors Associated with Working for an Employer That Offers a Plan

Table 14 shows the results of two models that analyze factors associated with the probability of working for an employer that offers (1) any type of pension plan (DB or DC) or (2) a DC plan. The first column presents the variables that were included in each model. The third and fifth columns present odds ratios that are estimated for each variable in the model.[5] The interpretation of the odds ratio for a particular variable depends on whether the variable has only two or more than two categories.[6] For dichotomous (or dummy) variables, odds ratios that are statistically significant and greater than 1.00 indicate that individuals with that characteristic are more likely to work for an employer that offers a plan. For example, an odds ratio of 1.25 for women would mean that women are 1.25 times more likely to work for an employer that offers a plan. Odds ratios that are significantly lower than 1.00 indicate that individuals with that characteristic are less likely to work for an employer that offers a plan. For categorical variables with more than two categories, a statistically significant odds ratio that is greater/less than 1.00 indicates that individuals in that category are more/less likely to work for an employer that offers a plan than individuals in the category that is chosen as the referent or comparison category.

As shown in the body of the report, before controlling for differences between men and women in demographic and occupational characteristics, a greater proportion of women worked for employers that offered plans in 2009. Interestingly, table 14 shows that after accounting for demographic and occupational characteristics, women have slightly lower odds of working for an employer that offers a DC plan than men. In fact, the positive gender effect for women is eliminated when we control for occupational characteristics using a statistical model (results not shown below). In other words, women's higher likelihood of working for an employer that offers a plan is largely due to the types of occupations and industries in which women work. (The odds ratios for the specific occupations and industries, which are too numerous to discuss here, are listed in the table.)

[5]Odds (O) are mathematically related to but not the same as probabilities (P), that is O=P/[1-P].

[6]While dummy and categorical variables are both discrete variables, a dummy variable takes on a value of 0 or 1. A categorical variable takes a value that is one of several possible categories and there is no intrinsic ordering to the categories.

We found that several other factors are associated with the likelihood of working for an employer that offers a plan. While the details are shown in the table, the factors that were positively associated with working for an employer that offers either a DB or DC plan (and that were statistically significant at the 95 percent confidence level) included age; being divorced (relative to married); education level; U.S. citizenship; working in the government or nonprofit sector (in comparison to the private sector); having 5 to 9 years of work experience (in comparison to having less than 5 years); union membership; job tenure; and firm size.

Factors that were negatively associated with working for an employer that offers a plan included being never married (in comparison to being married); being a single parent; being Black, Hispanic, or Asian (in comparison to White, non-Hispanics); being a naturalized immigrant; working part time; and being self-employed. While the results across both models were generally consistent, some results were significant in one model but not the other.

Table 14: Factors Associated with Working for an Employer That Offers a Plan, 2009

Dependent variable	Unadjusted proportion with employer that offers a DB or DC plan	Employer offers a DB or DC plan	Unadjusted proportion with employer that offers a DC plan	Employer offers a DC plan
Explanatory variables:				
Gender (omitted category is men)	58%		46%	
Women	61%	0.948	49%	0.938**
Age groups (omitted category age 18-24)	42%		33%	
25-34	60%	1.494***	49%	1.615***
35-44	62%	1.499***	50%	1.608***
45-54	64%	1.518***	51%	1.620***
55-64	63%	1.229***	48%	1.300***
Marital status (omitted category married)	63%		50%	
Widowed	59%	1.059	46%	1.083
Divorced	64%	1.135**	51%	1.097**
Separated	53%	1.008	42%	1.000
Never married	52%	0.906**	41%	0.965
Children in the household	59%	1.101**	47%	1.027
Single parent	49%	0.793***	39%	0.869**

Dependent variable	Unadjusted proportion with employer that offers a DB or DC plan	Employer offers a DB or DC plan	Unadjusted proportion with employer that offers a DC plan	Employer offers a DC plan
Race and ethnicity (omitted category White)	63%		51%	
Black, Non-Hispanic	61%	0.750***	46%	0.758***
Hispanic	43%	0.605***	32%	0.663***
Asian, Non-Hispanic	56%	0.761***	46%	0.882
Other, Non-Hispanic	59%	0.855*	47%	0.897
Education level (omitted category No high school diploma)	30%		24%	
High school diploma	51%	1.297***	39%	1.196***
Some college	61%	1.772***	48%	1.543***
Bachelor's degree or higher	72%	1.997***	57%	1.606***
Citizen	62%	1.577***	49%	1.499***
Naturalized immigrant	54%	0.737***	42%	0.787***
Part-time status (omitted category is full time)[a]	66%		52%	
Part-time	46%	0.763***	38%	0.925***
Sector (omitted category private sector)	60%		50%	
Private not for profit	73%	1.430***	59%	1.243***
Government worker	88%	2.142***	61%	1.062
Occupation (omitted category Management)	76%		64%	
Business and Financial Operations	82%	1.133	70%	1.053
Computer and Mathematical	85%	1.222*	73%	1.036
Architecture and Engineering	88%	1.737***	73%	1.196
Life, Physical, and Social Services	87%	1.067	68%	0.779*
Community and Social Services	74%	0.895	54%	0.701***
Legal	77%	1.139	66%	1.190
Education, Training, and Library	81%	0.605***	57%	0.600***
Arts, Design, Entertainment, Sports, and Media	64%	0.729**	52%	0.745**
Healthcare Practitioners and Technical	82%	1.314***	68%	1.003
Healthcare Support	57%	0.635***	46%	0.617***
Protective Service	77%	0.684***	54%	0.631***
Food Preparation and Serving Related	34%	0.530***	27%	0.524***
Building and Grounds Cleaning and Maintenance	42%	0.619***	30%	0.545***
Personal Care and Service	33%	0.326***	25%	0.363***
Sales and Related	60%	0.634***	49%	0.620***
Office and Administrative Support	69%	0.864*	55%	0.785***
Farming, Forestry, and Fishing	16%	0.265***	12%	0.290***

Dependent variable	Unadjusted proportion with employer that offers a DB or DC plan	Employer offers a DB or DC plan	Unadjusted proportion with employer that offers a DC plan	Employer offers a DC plan
Construction and Extraction	44%	0.690***	31%	0.595***
Installation, Repair, and Maintenance	66%	0.856	56%	0.929
Production	66%	0.607***	53%	0.628***
Transportation and Material Moving	61%	0.673***	48%	0.627***
Not in universe[b]	15%	0.894	10%	0.411***
Industry (omitted category Agriculture)	19%		16%	
Mining	69%	1.515	54%	1.235
Utilities	89%	3.134***	69%	1.785**
Construction	45%	1.379	33%	1.145
Manufacturing	76%	2.697***	63%	2.036***
Wholesale Trade	69%	2.725***	55%	1.923***
Retail Trade	62%	2.052***	51%	1.668**
Transportation and Warehousing	71%	1.763**	55%	1.525*
Information	76%	2.228***	63%	1.761**
Finance and Insurance	84%	3.571***	73%	2.614***
Real Estate and Rental and Leasing	49%	1.301	41%	1.255
Professional, Scientific, and Technical	71%	2.197***	61%	1.884***
Management, Administrative and Support	42%	1.059	34%	1.013
Educational Services	84%	2.120***	60%	1.461
Health Care and Social Assistance	67%	1.733**	55%	1.559*
Arts, Entertainment, and Recreation	51%	1.453	40%	1.268
Accommodations and Food Services	34%	0.996	28%	0.905
Other Services (Except Public Administration)	38%	1.144	30%	0.972
Public Administration	89%	2.198***	64%	1.499
Work experience (omitted category Less than 5 years)	56%		45%	
5 to 9 years	67%	1.140***	53%	1.069*
10 to 15 years	71%	1.033	56%	1.013
More than 15 years	57%	0.978	45%	0.989
Union status (omitted category not in a union)	63%		51%	
In a union	87%	1.903***	62%	1.094**
Self-employment status	19%	0.525***	14%	0.671***
Number of employees at current place of employment (omitted category Under 25 employees))	25%		19%	
25 to 100 employees	57%	3.291***	46%	3.021***
100+ employees	79%	7.618***	63%	5.528***

Dependent variable	Unadjusted proportion with employer that offers a DB or DC plan	Employer offers a DB or DC plan	Unadjusted proportion with employer that offers a DC plan	Employer offers a DC plan
Years of tenure at current job		1.042***	9%	1.015***
Tenure categories				
Less than 5 years	56%		45%	
5 to 9 years	69%		54%	
10 to 15 years	76%		60%	
More than 15 years	82%		63%	
Number of observations		37,038		37,038

Source: GAO analysis of SIPP data.

*Indicates that the variable is statistically significant at the 90 percent level.

**Indicates that the variable is statistically significant at the 95 percent level.

***Indicates that the variable is statistically significant at the 99 percent level.

[a]Part-time status is defined as working 35 hours or less per week during the reference period.

[b]The category "Not in universe" includes self-employed individuals.

Factors Associated with Eligibility for Employer-Sponsored Pension Plan

Table 15 shows the results of a model we estimated to analyze factors associated with whether an individual is eligible for their employer's plan. It is presented in the same format as table 14. As shown in the body of the report, women had lower rates of plan eligibility across all 4 study years. The results of the model show that, even after controlling for demographic and occupational differences between men and women, women had significantly lower rates of eligibility in 2009. Perhaps most interesting is the odds ratio for part-time status, which indicates that part-time workers are approximately one-third as likely to be eligible for their employer's plan as full-time workers. In addition, work experience and tenure are also significantly and positively related with eligibility. Union status is also positively associated with plan eligibility.

Table 15: Factors Associated with Eligibility for Employer-Sponsored Pension Plan, 2009

Dependent variable	Unadjusted proportion eligible for a DB or DC plan	Individual is eligible for a DB or DC plan
Gender (omitted category is men)	91%	
Women	87%	0.861**
Age groups (omitted category age 18-24)	55%	
25-34	88%	2.589***
35-44	93%	2.957***
45-54	94%	2.846***
55-64	93%	2.106***
Marital status (omitted category married)	92%	
Widowed	88%	0.637**
Divorced	92%	1.021
Separated	89%	0.998
Never married	77%	0.795***
Children in the household	89%	0.906
Single parent	77%	0.963
Race and ethnicity (omitted category White)	89%	
Black, Non-Hispanic	87%	0.998
Hispanic	87%	1.028
Asian, Non-Hispanic	90%	1.011
Other, Non-Hispanic	86%	1.023
Education level (omitted category No high school diploma)	82%	
High school diploma	87%	0.881
Some college	86%	0.872
Bachelor's degree or higher	93%	1.128
Citizen	89%	1.235
Naturalized immigrant	91%	0.886
Part-time status (omitted category is full time)[a]	94%	
Part-time	73%	0.315***
Sector (omitted category private sector)	87%	
Private not for profit	87%	0.867
Government worker	92%	0.996
Occupation (omitted category Management)	96%	
Business and Financial Operations	95%	0.958
Computer and Mathematical	95%	0.941
Architecture and Engineering	96%	1.088
Life, Physical, and Social Services	95%	0.924

Dependent variable	Unadjusted proportion eligible for a DB or DC plan	Individual is eligible for a DB or DC plan
Community and Social Services	90%	0.579**
Legal	94%	0.823
Education, Training, and Library	88%	0.492***
Arts, Design, Entertainment, Sports, and Media	87%	0.535**
Healthcare Practitioners and Technical	90%	0.595***
Healthcare Support	79%	0.346***
Protective Service	92%	0.533***
Food Preparation and Serving Related	65%	0.395***
Building and Grounds Cleaning and Maintenance	83%	0.396***
Personal Care and Service	69%	0.299***
Sales and Related	81%	0.466***
Office and Administrative Support	87%	0.474***
Farming, Forestry, and Fishing	89%	0.598
Construction and Extraction	92%	0.693
Installation, Repair, and Maintenance	93%	0.638**
Production	92%	0.482***
Transportation and Material Moving	85%	0.417***
Not in universe[b]	96%	1.461
Industry (omitted category Agriculture)	90%	
Mining	92%	0.765
Utilities	98%	1.572
Construction	91%	0.684
Manufacturing	94%	1.055
Wholesale Trade	92%	1.090
Retail Trade	79%	0.682
Transportation and Warehousing	90%	0.717
Information	91%	0.952
Finance and Insurance	92%	1.006
Real Estate and Rental and Leasing	89%	0.907
Professional, Scientific, and Technical	93%	0.854
Management, Administrative and Support	85%	0.656
Educational Services	88%	0.599
Health Care and Social Assistance	88%	0.831
Arts, Entertainment, and Recreation	75%	0.462
Accommodations and Food Services	67%	0.538
Other Services (Except Public Administration)	86%	0.738

Dependent variable	Unadjusted proportion eligible for a DB or DC plan	Individual is eligible for a DB or DC plan
Public Administration	95%	1.076
Work experience (omitted category Less than 5 years)	78%	
5 to 9 years	92%	1.419***
10 to 15 years	95%	1.435***
More than 15 years	92%	0.895*
Union status (omitted category not in a union)	87%	
In a union	95%	2.070***
Self-employment status	91%	0.864
Number of employees at current place of employment (omitted category Under 25 employees)	85%	
25 to 100 employees	88%	1.165*
100+ employees	89%	1.300***
Years of tenure at current job		1.169***
Tenure categories		
Less than 5 years	78%	
5 to 9 years	93%	
10 to 15 years	97%	
More than 15 years	99%	
Number of observations		24,274

Source: GAO analysis of SIPP data.

*Indicates that the variable is statistically significant at the 90 percent level.

**Indicates that the variable is statistically significant at the 95 percent level.

***Indicates that the variable is statistically significant at the 99 percent level.

[a]Part-time status is defined as working 35 hours or less per week during the reference period.

[b]The category "Not in universe" includes self-employed individuals.

Factors Associated with Participation in an Employer-Sponsored Pension Plan

Table 16 shows the results of two models we estimated to analyze factors associated with the probability of participating in (1) any type of pension plan (DB or DC) or (2) a DC plan. Again, it is presented in the same format as tables 14 and 15.

As shown in the body of the report, before controlling for differences between men and women in demographic and occupational characteristics, a smaller proportion of women participated in an employer-sponsored pension plan. Our analysis shows that the gender differences in plan participation are largely accounted for by differences between men and women in demographic and occupational characteristics.

Similar to our other models, we identify a number of factors that are related to plan participation. The factors that were positively related to participating in either a DB or a DC (and that are statistically significant at the 95 percent level) include age; education-level; being Asian (relative to whites); U.S. citizenship; working in the nonprofit or government sector (relative to the private sector); work-experience; union membership; and tenure. Factors that were negatively related to participating in a plan included being a single parent; working part-time; and being Black or Hispanic. A number of industries and occupations, too numerous to list, were statistically significant as shown in the table below.

Table 16: Factors Associated with Participation in an Employer-Sponsored Pension Plan, 2009

Dependent variable	Unadjusted proportion participating in a DB or DC plan	Individual participates in a DB or DC plan	Unadjusted proportion participating in a DC plan	Individual participates in a DC plan
Gender (omitted category is men)	87%		79%	
Women	86%	0.973	78%	1.099*
Age groups (omitted category age 18-24)	63%		54%	
25-34	83%	1.547***	75%	1.659***
35-44	87%	1.627***	80%	1.821***
45-54	91%	1.843***	83%	1.924***
55-64	92%	1.691***	82%	1.642***
Marital status (omitted category married)	90%		82%	
Widowed	90%	1.173	82%	1.129
Divorced	86%	0.867	78%	0.911
Separated	79%	0.871	68%	0.784
Never married	78%	0.888	71%	0.961
Children in the household	87%	1.125	79%	1.138*
Single parent	76%	0.805**	68%	0.844*
Race and ethnicity (omitted category White)	88%		81%	
Black, Non-Hispanic	81%	0.705***	68%	0.579***
Hispanic	77%	0.684***	69%	0.737***
Asian, Non-Hispanic	90%	1.304*	85%	1.500***
Other, Non-Hispanic	86%	1.108	77%	0.950
Education level (omitted category No high school diploma)	69%		61%	
High school diploma	82%	1.275**	72%	1.190
Some college	85%	1.617***	77%	1.548***
Bachelor's degree or higher	92%	2.318***	84%	1.871***
Citizen	87%	1.619***	79%	1.570***

Dependent variable	Unadjusted proportion participating in a DB or DC plan	Individual participates in a DB or DC plan	Unadjusted proportion participating in a DC plan	Individual participates in a DC plan
Naturalized immigrant	87%	0.991	80%	1.055
Part-time status (omitted category is full time)[a]	88%		80%	
Part-time	81%	0.791***	74%	0.851***
Sector (omitted category private sector)	83%		77%	
Private not for profit	88%	1.274***	80%	1.219***
Government worker	94%	1.902***	82%	1.239**
Occupation (omitted category Management)	92%		87%	
Business and Financial Operations	91%	0.885	85%	0.847
Computer and Mathematical	91%	0.823	86%	0.790
Architecture and Engineering	94%	1.256	89%	0.969
Life, Physical, and Social Services	96%	1.387	90%	1.147
Community and Social Services	88%	0.636**	82%	0.808
Legal	92%	0.883	86%	0.856
Education, Training, and Library	92%	0.606***	79%	0.520***
Arts, Design, Entertainment, Sports, and Media	86%	0.661*	79%	0.609**
Healthcare Practitioners and Technical	87%	0.712**	80%	0.694**
Healthcare Support	75%	0.545***	64%	0.457***
Protective Service	93%	0.727	80%	0.713**
Food Preparation and Serving Related	63%	0.556***	53%	0.488***
Building and Grounds Cleaning and Maintenance	76%	0.570***	63%	0.542***
Personal Care and Service	73%	0.516***	63%	0.483***
Sales and Related	82%	0.734**	75%	0.678***
Office and Administrative Support	84%	0.576***	76%	0.574***
Farming, Forestry, and Fishing	82%	0.913	78%	1.014
Construction and Extraction	89%	0.914	79%	0.681*
Installation, Repair, and Maintenance	85%	0.627***	77%	0.613***
Production	82%	0.476***	75%	0.523***
Transportation and Material Moving	83%	0.723**	73%	0.650***
Not in universe[b]	94%	2.604*	88%	0.765
Industry (omitted category Agriculture)	76%		72%	
Mining	94%	5.874***	91%	5.571***
Utilities	94%	3.325***	84%	1.871*
Construction	89%	2.673***	81%	2.222**
Manufacturing	88%	2.907***	82%	2.401***
Wholesale Trade	86%	2.567**	82%	2.330**
Retail Trade	77%	1.770*	69%	1.435
Transportation and Warehousing	87%	1.937*	77%	1.683
Information	88%	2.520**	82%	2.107**
Finance and Insurance	92%	4.287***	86%	2.868***
Real Estate and Rental and Leasing	77%	1.346	68%	1.120
Professional, Scientific, and Technical	89%	2.555***	84%	2.059**

Dependent variable	Unadjusted proportion participating in a DB or DC plan	Individual participates in a DB or DC plan	Unadjusted proportion participating in a DC plan	Individual participates in a DC plan
Management, Administrative and Support	74%	1.511	68%	1.291
Educational Services	92%	2.231**	80%	1.612
Health Care and Social Assistance	83%	1.824*	76%	1.513
Arts, Entertainment, and Recreation	75%	1.253	66%	1.117
Accommodations and Food Services	60%	1.057	55%	1.017
Other Services (Except Public Administration)	81%	1.845*	71%	1.183
Public Administration	96%	4.284***	85%	1.868*
Work experience (omitted category Less than 5 years)	77%		69%	
5 to 9 years	85%	1.150**	77%	1.185**
10 to 15 years	89%	1.250***	82%	1.305***
More than 15 years	91%	1.195**	84%	1.250***
Union status (omitted category not in a union)	85%			
In a union	93%	1.579***	80%	0.980
Self-employment status	91%	1.020	85%	0.860
Number of employees at current place of employment (omitted category Under 25 employees)	83%		79%	
25 to 100 employees	82%	0.916	77%	0.878
100+ employees	87%	1.172*	79%	0.936
Years of tenure at current job		1.084***		1.036***
Tenure categories				
Less than 5 years	77%		69%	
5 to 9 years	87%		80%	
10 to 15 years	92%		85%	
More than 15 years	96%		87%	
Number of observations		21,494		17,067

Source: GAO analysis of SIPP data.

*Indicates that the variable is statistically significant at the 90 percent level.

**Indicates that the variable is statistically significant at the 95 percent level.

***Indicates that the variable is statistically significant at the 99 percent level.

[a]Part-time status is defined as working 35 hours or less per week during the reference period.

[b]The category "Not in universe" includes self-employed individuals.

Section 3: Methods for Comparing the Income of Women and Men Age 65 and Over

To compute median incomes and income composition for men and women in different demographic groups, we used information from the core questionnaire of the SIPP data (as described above). We used the last month of the 4-month reporting period (within each "wave") with the assumption that individuals will more accurately recollect income from the most recent month than income from 4 months ago. To obtain an annual income estimate, we multiplied the monthly reported income by 12.[7]

The poverty rate was computed using a SIPP variable that indicates the poverty threshold for an individual's household. The Census Bureau uses a set of money-income thresholds that vary by family size and composition to determine who is in poverty. If a family's total income is less than the family's threshold, then that family and every individual in it is considered in poverty. The official poverty thresholds do not vary geographically, but they are updated for inflation using Consumer Price Index (CPI-U). The official poverty definition uses money income before taxes and does not include capital gains or noncash benefits (such as public housing, Medicaid, and food stamps).

All of our income composition, median, and poverty level estimates were computed at the individual level, using household-level information. In other words, median incomes were computed by applying all household income to each individual in the household and taking the median across all individuals within a certain category (e.g., gender, or gender and race). For married individuals, this means that spousal income was included in these estimates. Correspondingly, we used SIPP individual-level weights to compute our point estimates and, in conjunction with other factors, calculate the standard errors of those estimates so that we could accurately account for the complex survey design.

The point estimates for household income for married men and married women may not be equal for a couple of reasons. First, the criteria for including an individual in the sample in our analysis was that he or she was 65 or above. While there are more women than men among all people over 65 in our sample, among married people over 65 there are more men than women.[8] One reason this might occur is due to

---

[7] This method might result in overstated estimates from earnings if workers do not work all 12 months of the year.

[8] These patterns held across all the years we analyzed.

demographic patterns of life-expectancy and the ages of marital partners.[9] Since women typically marry older men, and women typically have longer life-expectancies than men, it is not surprising that a sample of older individuals will include fewer married women than married men, as the spouses of older women are more likely to have died than the spouses of older men. For this reason, the sample of married older women could differ from the sample of married older men, so their household characteristics—including income—may not be the same. Further, the difference between the ages of the spouses of married men and married women could also result in different estimates of median income and income composition. For example, if women tended to be married to older men, the income composition of the household might be skewed away from earnings and towards Social Security. Conversely, if men tended to be married to younger women, a higher share of income might come from earnings.

Section 4: Methods for Analyzing the Effects of Events Occurring Later in Life on Women's and Men's Household Income and Assets

We estimated the relationship between events that occur later in life and income and assets using fixed-effects panel regressions. The main advantage of fixed-effects models is that they are designed to isolate the effect of the event from all other permanent characteristics of the individual. We estimated our models using data from the HRS, which follows households over time. Our analysis focuses on life events that occur after age 50, as the HRS follows individuals age 51 and over.

Descriptive Analysis of the Frequency of Life Events by Gender

Prior to analyzing the effect of the life events on assets and income, we first estimated the differences in the frequency of life events by gender. We estimated these differences in two ways. First, we estimated the proportion of women and men that had a life event across all the periods (e.g., proportion that were divorced). Second, we estimated the proportion of women and men that had that life event change between two periods

---

[9]It is also possible that the survey response rate was higher for married men than for married women.

of observation (e.g., proportion that became divorced between period 1 and period 2).

Table 19 uses the first method and presents some descriptive statistics on the women and men in our sample. Specifically, it shows the average values of characteristics for different ages for women and men.

- *Real assets and real income.* At ages 51 to 64 women and men have similar levels of assets. However, after age 65, men's average level of household assets becomes larger than the average level for women. Men's average levels of household income are higher than women's at every age level.

- *Marital status.* The rates of marriage and widowhood are relatively comparable between women and men before age 65. For example, 6 percent of women and 1 percent of men younger than age 65 were widowed. However, at older ages, more women were estimated to be widowed than men.

- *Poor health.* Individuals were classified as being in poor health based on a survey question of self-reported health, which asked the individual to rate his or her health on a scale from 1 to 5, where 1 is excellent and 5 is poor. An answer of "fair" or "poor" was classified as being in poor health. As table 17 shows, rates of poor health were comparable between women and men at all age groups.

- *Unemployment.* This variable captures the percentage of individuals that responded to a labor force question as being "unemployed". It is important to note that this is not equivalent to an unemployment rate—as individuals classified as not in the labor force were included in the denominator. Women and men were equally likely to report being unemployed.

- *Helping parents financially or with daily activities.* These variables capture the percentage of households that provided financial help or assistance with basic daily activities to either the parents of the respondent or spouse. Again, it appears that these rates were comparable for women and men.

Table 17: Descriptive Statistics of Women and Men in the HRS by Age

	Age	Estimate	Standard error	Lower bound of 95 percent confidence interval	Upper bound of 95 percent confidence interval	Error over estimate
Women						
Mean real household assets	Under age 51	$446,436	$18,911	$409,372	$483,500	4.24%
	Ages 51-64	$537,262	$9,039	$519,546	$554,978	1.68%
	Ages 65-84	$522,190	$6,020	$510,391	$533,989	1.15%
	Ages 85-99	$359,269	$12,341	$335,071	$383,447	3.44%
Mean real household income	Under age 51	$128,325	$6,899	$114,803	$141,847	5.38%
	Ages 51-64	$98,116	$1,185	$95,794	$100,438	1.21%
	Ages 65-84	$55,014	$348	$54,332	$55,696	0.63%
	Ages 85-99	$32,728	$746	$31,275	$34,201	2.28%
Percent married	Under age 51	87%	0.46%	86%	88%	0.52%
	Ages 51-64	78%	0.19%	78%	78%	0.24%
	Ages 65-84	64%	0.20%	63%	64%	0.32%
	Ages 85-99	23%	0.48%	22%	24%	2.05%
Percent divorced or separated	Under age 51	6%	0.33%	5%	6%	5.67%
	Ages 51-64	12%	0.16%	12%	13%	1.27%
	Ages 65-84	8%	0.12%	7%	8%	1.55%
	Ages 85-99	4%	0.23%	4%	5%	5.71%
Percent widowed	Under age 51	1%	0.11%	0%	1%	16.19%
	Ages 51-64	6%	0.10%	6%	6%	1.74%
	Ages 65-84	26%	0.19%	26%	26%	0.72%
	Ages 85-99	70%	0.53%	69%	71%	0.76%
Percent in poor health	Under age 51	15%	0.45%	14%	16%	3.01%
	Ages 51-64	21%	0.18%	21%	21%	0.87%
	Ages 65-84	28%	0.19%	28%	29%	0.66%
	Ages 85-99	40%	0.57%	39%	41%	1.41%
Percent unemployed	Under age 51	3%	0.22%	3%	3%	7.34%
	Ages 51-64	2%	0.06%	2%	2%	3.48%
	Ages 65-84	0.1%	0.01%	0%	0%	13.11%
	Ages 85-99	0%	0.01%	0%	0%	100.00%
Percent who helped their parents financially	Under age 51	16%	0.48%	15%	17%	3.00%
	Ages 51-64	11%	0.15%	11%	11%	1.33%
	Ages 65-84	2%	0.06%	2%	2%	3.06%
	Ages 85-99	0.1%	0.03%	0%	0%	48.61%
Percent who helped their parents with daily activities	Under age 51	8%	0.34%	7%	8%	4.56%
	Ages 51-64	9%	0.13%	9%	9%	1.51%
	Ages 65-84	3%	0.07%	2%	3%	2.70%
	Ages 85-99	0.1%	0.03%	0%	0%	52.68%

	Age	Estimate	Standard error	Lower bound of 95 percent confidence interval	Upper bound of 95 percent confidence interval	Error over estimate
Men						
Mean real household assets	Under age 51	$369,106	$19,9401	$330,023	$408,189	5.40%
	Ages 51-64	$540,761	$9,581	$521,982	$559,541	1.77%
	Ages 65-84	$638,166	$8,352	$621,796	$654,537	1.31%
	Ages 85-99	$528,611	$17,682	$493,955	$563,268	3.35%
Mean real household income	Under age 51	$107,801	$3,371	$101,194	$114,409	3.13%
	Ages 51-64	$112,785	$1,726	$109,402	$116,168	1.53%
	Ages 65-84	$72,767	$1,718	$69,400	$76,133	2.36%
	Ages 85-99	$48,073	$1,023	$46,068	$50,078	2.13%
Percent married	Under age 51	76%	1.25%	74%	79%	1.63%
	Ages 51-64	83%	0.20%	83%	84%	0.24%
	Ages 65-84	85%	0.17%	85%	85%	0.19%
	Ages 85-99	71%	0.62%	70%	72%	0.87%
Percent Divorced or Separated	Under age 51	9%	0.85%	7%	11%	9.61%
	Ages 51-64	10%	0.17%	10%	11%	1.60%
	Ages 65-84	6%	0.11%	5%	6%	2.02%
	Ages 85-99	2%	0.21%	2%	3%	8.62%
Percent widowed	Under age 51	0.1%	0.10%	0%	0%	70.66%
	Ages 51-64	1%	0.06%	1%	2%	4.24%
	Ages 65-84	7%	0.11%	6%	7%	1.66%
	Ages 85-99	24%	0.59%	23%	26%	2.41%
Percent in poor health	Under age 51	18%	1.11%	15%	20%	6.34%
	Ages 51-64	20%	0.20%	20%	21%	0.98%
	Ages 65-84	28%	0.19%	28%	29%	0.68%
	Ages 85-99	40%	0.66%	39%	41%	1.65%
Percent unemployed	Under age 51	3%	0.49%	2%	4%	15.70%
	Ages 51-64	2%	0.07%	2%	2%	3.58%
	Ages 65-84	0.2%	0.02%	0%	0%	9.73%
	Ages 85-99	0%	0.00%	0%	0%	.
Percent who helped their parents financially	Under age 51	17%	1.14%	15%	20%	6.56%
	Ages 51-64	13%	0.17%	13%	13%	1.34%
	Ages 65-84	4%	0.09%	4%	4%	2.26%
	Ages 85-99	0.2%	0.06%	0%	0%	28.54%
Percent who helped their parents with daily activities	Under age 51	10%	0.91%	8%	12%	9.17%
	Ages 51-64	9%	0.14%	8%	9%	1.67%
	Ages 65-84	4%	0.09%	4%	4%	2.27%
	Ages 85-99	0.3%	0.10%	0%	1%	28.65%

Source: GAO analysis of HRS data.

Table 18 uses the second method to show the proportion of women and men that had a life event status change during the period of analysis. As table 18 shows:

- *Divorce/separation.* During the period in which both members of the household are less than 65, less than 1 percent of men experienced divorce or separation between any of the two waves. For women, the proportion was negative – indicating that more women went from divorced or separated to married than from married to divorced or separated.

- *Widowhood.* During the earlier period, about 1 percent of women became widowed between any of the two waves. This proportion increased to more than 2 percent as the household aged and was twice the rate for men.

- *Decline into poor health.* The rate of health decline was similar for women and men. On average, approximately 2 percent of women and men reported a decline in health from one period to another.

- *Unemployment.* Very few women and men reported a change to and from unemployment in our data.

- *Helping parents financially or with daily activities.* The proportion of women's and men's households providing personal or financial assistance fell as the household aged. This may be because older households were less likely to have living parents requiring assistance.

- *Percent change in real assets.* In the earlier period, assets for women and men increased at a rate of about 6 percent per 2-year period. Alternatively, the rate of asset growth became negative as the household aged.

- *Percent change in real income.* In both younger and older households, incomes fell at a rate of approximately 5 percent per 2-year period, on average.

Table 18: Proportion of Individuals Changing Status between Observations

	Household type	Estimate	Standard error	Lower bound of 95 percent confidence interval	Upper bound of 95 percent confidence interval	Error over estimate
Women						
Divorced or separated	Households where everyone is age 64 or younger	-0.0022	0.0008	-0.0038	-0.0007	(35.40%)
	Households where at least one person is 65 or over	-0.0011	0.0005	-0.002	-0.0001	(46.32%)
	All households	-0.0016	0.0005	-0.0025	-0.0007	(28.13%)
Widowhood	Households where everyone is age 64 or younger	0.0106	0.0007	0.0094	0.0119	6.13%
	Households where at least one person is 65 or over	0.0237	0.0007	0.0223	0.0251	3.05%
	All households	0.0177	0.0005	0.0168	0.0187	2.79%
Decline in health	Households where everyone is age 64 or younger	0.0128	0.0019	0.009	0.0165	14.93%
	Households where at least one person is 65 or over	0.026	0.0016	0.0229	0.0291	6.07%
	All households	0.02	0.0012	0.0176	0.0224	6.12%
Unemployment	Households where everyone is age 64 or younger	-0.0026	0.0011	-0.0047	-0.0005	(40.90%)
	Households where at least one person is 65 or over	-0.0003	0.0003	-0.001	0.0003	(90.77%)
	All households	-0.0014	0.0005	-0.0024	-0.0004	(37.43%)
Helped parents financially	Households where everyone is age 64 or younger	-0.0028	0.0018	-0.0064	0.0008	(65.46%)
	Households where at least one person is 65 or over	-0.006	0.0008	-0.0074	-0.0045	(12.81%)
	All households	-0.0045	0.0009	-0.0064	-0.0027	(20.76%)
Helped parents with daily activities	Households where everyone is age 64 or younger	0.0069	0.0019	0.0031	0.0107	27.91%
	Households where at least one person is 65 or over	-0.0048	0.0009	-0.0065	-0.0031	(18.32%)
	All households	0.0006	0.001	-0.0014	0.0025	177.50%
Real household assets	Households where everyone is age 64 or younger	0.0533	0.0058	0.0419	0.0646	10.87%
	Households where at least one person is 65 or over	-0.0361	0.004	-0.0439	-0.0283	(11.09%)
	All households	0.0041	0.0034	-0.0026	0.0107	84.14%

	Household type	Estimate	Standard error	Lower bound of 95 percent confidence interval	Upper bound of 95 percent confidence interval	Error over estimate
Real household income	Households where everyone is age 64 or younger	-0.0542	0.0051	-0.0642	-0.0441	(9.448%)
	Households where at least one person is 65 or over	-0.054	0.0027	-0.0593	-0.0487	(4.992%)
	All households	-0.0541	0.0028	-0.0595	-0.0487	(5.085%)
Men						
Divorced or separated	Households where everyone is age 64 or younger	0.0007	0.0009	-0.0011	0.0025	126.10%
	Households where at least one person is 65 or over	0.0009	0.0005	0	0.0019	52.34%
	All households	0.0008	0.0005	-0.0002	0.0019	62.40%
Widowhood	Households where everyone is age 64 or younger	0.003	0.0005	0.002	0.004	17.07%
	Households where at least one person is 65 or over	0.0133	0.0006	0.0122	0.0145	4.46%
	All households	0.0082	0.0004	0.0074	0.009	4.79%
Decline in health	Households where everyone is age 64 or younger	0.0171	0.0021	0.013	0.0212	12.33%
	Households where at least one person is 65 or over	0.0348	0.0019	0.0311	0.0384	5.39%
	All households	0.026	0.0014	0.0232	0.0288	5.42%
Unemployment	Households where everyone is age 64 or younger	-0.0002	0.0011	-0.0024	0.002	(513.2%)
	Households where at least one person is 65 or over	0	0.0003	-0.0007	0.0006	(4975%)
	All households	-0.0001	0.0006	-0.0012	0.001	(520.0%)
Helped parents financially	Households where everyone is age 64 or younger	-0.0021	0.002	-0.0061	0.0019	(95.72%)
	Households where at least one person is 65 or over	-0.0068	0.001	-0.0087	-0.0049	(14.16%)
	All households	-0.0045	0.0011	-0.0067	-0.0023	(24.88%)
Helped parents with daily activities	Households where everyone is age 64 or younger	0.0061	0.002	0.0022	0.0101	32.59%
	Households where at least one person is 65 or over	-0.0042	0.0011	-0.0063	-0.0021	(25.43%)
	All households	0.0009	0.0011	-0.0013	0.0031	120.90%

	Household type	Estimate	Standard error	Lower bound of 95 percent confidence interval	Upper bound of 95 percent confidence interval	Error over estimate
Real household assets	Households where everyone is age 64 or younger	0.0566	0.0061	0.0447	0.0684	10.70%
	Households where at least one person is 65 or over	-0.0268	0.0041	-0.0349	-0.0188	(15.37%)
	All households	0.0137	0.0036	0.0066	0.0209	26.41%
Real household income	Households where everyone is age 64 or younger	-0.0486	0.0052	-0.0587	-0.0385	(10.60%)
	Households where at least one person is 65 or over	-0.0536	0.0031	-0.0596	-0.0475	(5.767%)
	All households	-0.0511	0.003	-0.057	-0.0453	(5.835%)

Source: GAO analysis of HRS data.

Estimating the Effects of Events Occurring Later in Life on Assets and Income

In order to examine whether the effects of certain events occurring later in life differ by gender, we used fixed-effects regression models. For example, we estimated how changes in health lead to changes in household assets and income. Researchers use the fixed-effects method because much of the differences in income and wealth between households are consistent over time (as poorer households tend to stay poor and richer households tend to stay rich). The fixed-effects method sweeps away these "time invariant" differences, thus better isolating the effect of health or other life events from other aspects of households that could explain differences.[10]

---

[10] In addition to the fixed-effects analysis, we also developed "cross-section" regression models. In these models, we attempted to control for a set of demographic and other variables, such as education and age that could be correlated with life events, household assets, and household income. A challenge to this approach is that many factors that affect assets and income are unobserved, and lead to mistaken conclusions. For example, if an individual earns a low wage, that may be connected with poor health and the accumulation of assets. So, while the researcher is attempting to estimate the effect of health on income, what is actually measured is the effect of income on health. In general, in our cross-section models, we found that effects were larger in magnitude than in the fixed-effects models, but these models were not as good a fit to the data as the fixed-effects models.

Specifically, we estimated variations of the following equation, separately by gender:

(1) Log (Household Assets or Income) = α_i + α_t + β*(poor health) + χ *(marital status) + δ*(other control variables)

Where, α_i and α_t indicate fixed effects for the individual and wave. β is the effect of poor health and δ and χ are the effect of other control variables and marital status.[11] By including a dummy variable for each wave, we attempted to control for all national-level changes that could have affected assets and income, and also have been associated with the life events. Therefore, β can be interpreted as the effect of poor health, measured as the percent difference in average assets between periods where an individual reports poor versus not-poor health. Due to the additional controls, this average percent difference is measured relative to the changes over time, and also relative to the other time-variant measures captured, such as changes in marital status.[12]

However, while some of the life-events are likely associated with the passage of time, the regression does not assume that relationship. For example, if an individual switches from poor health to good health, the fixed-effects regression will also use those transitions to estimate the size of the effect. Similarly, the fixed-effects regression will also use transitions from married to widowed, as well as widowed to married, to estimate the effect of widowhood.

As is common among all regressions, a limitation of the fixed-effects method is that some important variable could be omitted from the model. While the fixed effect controls for all time-invariant attributes, there is still

---

[11]Other control variables that we included were age (measured as date of wave minus birth year), race and education (categorical), cohort of HRS survey, Census region, region of birth (12 categories, including non-U.S.). In general, in the cross-section models, we found that education was positively related to assets and income, while minority status was negatively related. With some slight variation, we based our choice of control variables on Coile and Milligan. (See Courtney Coile and Kevin Milligan, "How Household Portfolios Evolve After Retirement: The Effect of Aging and Health Shocks," *The Review of Income and Wealth*, vol. 55 no. 2 (Malden, MA: June 2009)).

[12]In order to estimate effects in terms of percents, we estimated the effects on the log of assets or income. In addition, we transformed the coefficients to more closely approximate percent changes by taking the exponent of the estimated coefficient and subtracting 1. Regression variables were weighted by household weights.

the possibility of endogenous relationships. For example, if an individual's health declined because income fell, and not the other way around, that bias could affect our findings.

Some of the life events we examined were likely correlated with changes in household structure, such as changes in marital status. However, if the income of a household falls when an individual leaves, the remaining individuals may not be worse off when it comes to resources because the household now requires fewer resources to meet its needs. To address this, we adjusted the estimated effects by household size; the household's income and assets were scaled by the square root of the individuals in the household. The rationale for using the square root is because the effect of reducing members is diminishing (changing from 1 to 2 has a larger effect than going from 9 to 10). In addition, this analysis estimated the effect of an individual's life event on household assets or income. We did not attempt to determine to what extent a spouse's life event (for married individuals) may have affected household assets or income).

Divorce

Table 19 contains the effects of the first event we analyzed: divorce. We analyzed the effect of divorce on household assets and income, both with and without controlling for the number of people in the household. Across almost all the groups and specifications, the effect of divorce is to reduce assets and income, with larger effects for women than for men. Adjusting for household size tended to reduce the magnitude of the effects.

- *Effect on assets.* Divorce tended to reduce assets for more women than men, with comparable sizes of effects for women and men. For example, among all households, the decline in assets associated with divorce was 41 percent for women and 39 percent for men. When the size of the household was adjusted for, the size of the effect declined, but was still statistically significant.

- *Effect on income.* Divorce reduced income for both women and men, with larger effects for women than men. For example, among all households, the decline in income associated with divorce was 41 percent for women and 23 percent for men. When household size was adjusted for, the size of the effects were much smaller in magnitude.

Table 19: Divorce Effect on Household Assets and Income

	All households		Households where everyone is age 64 or younger		Households where at least one person is 65 or over	
	Women	Men	Women	Men	Women	Men
Effect on assets						
Log point change	-0.53	-0.50	-0.54	-0.50	-0.39	-0.38
Standard error	(0.022)	(0.02)	(0.03)	(0.03)	(0.04)	(0.040)
Percent change	- 41%	-39%	- 41%	- 39%	- 32%	- 32%
Effects on assets per household member						
Log point change	-0.37	-0.32	-0.41	-0.32	-0.18	-0.24
Standard error	(0.022)	(0.022)	(0.03)	(0.03)	(0.04)	(0.04)
Percent change	- 31%	- 28%	- 33%	- 28%	- 17%	- 21%
Effect on income						
Log point change	-0.52	-0.26	- 0.58	-0.29	-0.49	-0.27
Standard error	(0.02)	(0.02)	(0.03)	(0.025)	(0.02)	(0.025)
Percent change	- 41%	- 23%	- 44%	- 25%	- 39%	- 23%
Effect on income per household member						
Log point change	-0.37	-0.09	-0.46	-0.12	-0.29	-0.13
Standard error	(0.02)	(0.02)	(0.03)	(0.03)	(0.020)	(0.025)
Percent change	- 31%	- 9%	- 37%	-11%	- 25%	- 12%

Source: GAO analysis of HRS data.

Widowhood

Table 20 contains the results for widowhood. As with divorce, we analyzed the effect of widowhood on household assets and income, both with and without controlling for the number of people in the household. Across almost all the groups and specifications, the effect of widowhood is to reduce assets and income, with larger effects for women than for men. Adjusting for household size tended to reduce the magnitude of the effects.

- *Effect on assets.* Widowhood reduced assets for both women and men, with larger effects for women than men. For example, among all households, the decline in assets associated with widowhood was 32 percent for women and 27 percent for men. However, part of this effect seems to be associated with the size of the household. Among the households in which at least one member was 65 and over, the decline in assets was not significant when household size was adjusted for.

- *Effect on income.* Widowhood reduced income for both women and men, with larger effects for women than men. For example, among all households, the decline in income associated with widowhood was 37 percent for women and 22 percent for men. Again, part of this effect seems to be associated with the size of the household. When household size was adjusted for, the size of the effects were much smaller in magnitude.

Table 20: Widowhood Effect on Household Assets and Income

	All households		Households where everyone is age 64 or younger		Households where at least one person is 65 or over	
	Women	Men	Women	Men	Women	Men
Effect on assets						
Log point change	-0.39	-0.31	-0.37	-0.26	-0.26	-0.20
Standard error	(0.01)	(0.02)	(0.034)	(0.051)	(0.02)	(0.02)
Percent change	-32%	-27%	-31%	-23%	-23%	-18%
Effect on assets per household member						
Log point change	-0.19	-0.11	-0.20	-0.03	-0.02	-0.00
Standard error	(0.01)	(0.02)	(0.03)	(0.05)	(0.02)	(0.02)
Percent change	-17%	-10%	-18%	-3%	-2%	- .3%
Effect on income						
Log point change	-0.46	-0.25	-0.63	-0.36	-0.43	-0.23
Standard error	(0.01)	(0.02)	(0.03)	(0.04)	(0.01)	(0.01)
Percent change	-37%	-22%	-47%	-30%	-35%	-21%
Effect on income per household member						
Log point change	-0.27	-0.06	-0.48	-0.17	- 0.20	- 0.04
Standard error	(0.01)	(0.02)	(0.03)	(0.04)	(0.01)	(0.02)
Percent change	-23%	-6%	-38%	-16%	-18%	-4%

Source: GAO analysis of HRS data.

Unemployment

As shown in table 21, unemployment tended to reduce assets and income, with comparable effects for women and men. The effects did not seem to dissipate when household size was adjusted for.

- *Effect on assets.* Unemployment reduced assets for both women and men, with comparable effects for women and men. For example, among all households, the decline in assets associated with unemployment was 7 percent for women and 7 percent for men. An exception to this difference was in cases in which at least one member was 65 or over. For those individuals, the decline in household assets was only 2 percent for women and 15 percent for men.

- *Effect on income.* Unemployment reduced income for both women and men, with comparable effects for women and men. For example, among all households, the decline in income associated with unemployment was 6 percent for women and 8 percent for men.

Table 21: Unemployment Effect

	All households		Households where everyone is age 64 or younger		Households where at least one person is 65 or over	
	Women	Men	Women	Men	Women	Men
Effect on assets						
Log point change	-0.07	-0.07	-0.09	-0.07	-0.02	-0.15
Standard error	(0.02)	(0.02)	(0.03)	(0.03)	(0.07)	(0.075)
Percent change	-7%	-7%	-9%	-7%	-2%	-14%
Effects on assets per household member						
Log point change	-0.06	-0 .08	-0.08	-0.08	-0 .03	-0 .16
Standard error	(0.02)	(0.02)	(0.03)	(0.03)	(0.07)	(0.076)
Percent change	-6%	-8%	-8%	-8%	-3%	-15%
Effects on income						
Log point change	-0.09	-0.07	-0.10	-0.06	-0.13	-0.12
Standard error	(0.02)	(0.02)	(0.02)	(0.02)	(0.04)	(0.05)
Percent change	-9%	-7%	-9%	-6%	-13%	-12%
Effects on income per household member						
Log point change	-0.09	-0.08	-0.09	-0.07	-0.14	-0.13
Standard error	(0.02)	(0.02)	(0.02)	(0.02)	(0.04)	(0.05)
Percent change	-8%	-7%	-8%	-7%	-13%	-12%

Source: GAO analysis of HRS data.

A Decline in Health

In general, across the specifications, the effect of a decline into poor health tended to reduce assets and income, with comparable effects for women and men (see table 22). One notable difference however, were the larger estimated effects of men's poor health on assets, but only in the case where both members of the household were less than 65 years of age. Specifically, we found that for individuals living in these households, poor health in men was associated with a drop in household assets of 13 percent, but 5 percent for women.[13]

In general, the magnitude of the effect on assets was in the 10 percent range for both women and men, and is statistically significant. The effects on income are about half that magnitude, but follow the same direction as the effects on assets. There is little difference in the effects when the level of assets and income are estimated with a correction for the size of the household.

Table 22: A Decline in Health's Effect on Household Assets and Income

	All households		Households where everyone is age 64 or younger		Households where at least one person is 65 or over	
	Women	Men	Women	Men	Women	Men
Effect on assets						
Log point change	-0.09	-0.10	-0.05	-0.14	-0.06	-0.04
Standard error	(0.008)	(0.008)	(0.01)	(0.01)	(0.01)	(0.01)
Percent change	-8%	-10%	-5%	-13%	-6%	-4%
Effects on assets per household member						
Log point change	-0.09	-0.11	-0.06	-0.14	-0.06	-0.05
Standard error	(0.008)	(0.008)	(0.01)	(0.01)	(0.01)	(0.01)
Percent change	-9%	-10%	-5%	-13%	-6%	-5%
Effect on income						
Log point change	-0.04	-0.03	-0.05	-0.03	-0.03	-0.02
Standard error	(0.006)	(0.006)	(0.01)	(0.01)	(0.01)	(0.01)
Percent change	-4%	-3%	-5%	-3%	-3%	-2%
Effect on income per household member						
Log point change	-0.05	-0.04	-0.05	-0.03	-0.03	-0.02
Standard error	(0.006)	(0.006)	(0.01)	(0.01)	(0.01)	(0.01)
Percent change	-5%	-4%	-5%	-3%	-3%	-2%

Source: GAO analysis of HRS data.

[13]We tested this result by using an alternative measure of health: the extent to which there are challenges in daily living. In this case, we did not find that men's health had a larger effect.

Helping Parents Financially or with Daily Activities

As shown in table 23, the results for either helping parents financially or with basic daily activities—eating, dressing, and bathing—were not as consistently significantly negative as the other life events. In the fixed-effects regression, the effect of personal assistance did not appear to be statistically significant, while the effect of financial assistance tended to be significantly positive. It may be that when households have more assets or income they are more likely to provide assistance—which could explain these findings. There is little difference in the effects when the level of assets and income are estimated with a correction for the size of the household. To further understand these relationships, we explored the characteristics of those helping their parents with the basic daily activities of bathing, dressing, and eating. We found that only 2 percent of the sample provided both financial help and help with basic daily activities. Further, those in the labor force (i.e., working or unemployed and looking for work) were more likely to help their parents with basic daily activities than those retired or not in the labor force.

Table 23: Effects of Providing Financial Assistance or Physical Care on Household Assets and Income

	Helped parents financially		Helped parents with basic daily activities	
	Women	Men	Women	Men
Effect on assets				
Log point change	0.028	0.034	0.0	0.01
Standard error	(0.01)	(0.01)	(0.01)	(0.01)
Percent change	3%	3%	1%	1%
Effects on assets per household member				
Log point change	0.032	0.038	0.004	0.01
Standard error	(0.01)	(0.01)	(0.01)	(0.02)
Percent change	3%	4%	0.4%	1%
Effect on income				
Log point change	0.056	0.071	0.016	0.020
Standard error	(0.008)	(0.008)	(0.008)	(0.008)
Percent change	6%	7%	2%	2%
Effect on income per household member				
Log point change	0.059	0.073	0.013	0.018
Standard error	(0.008)	(0.008)	(0.008)	(0.008)
Percent change	6%	8%	1%	2%

Source: GAO analysis of HRS data.

Appendix II: GAO Contact and Staff Acknowledgments

GAO Contact	Charles Jeszeck, (202) 512-7215 or jeszeckc@gao.gov
Staff Acknowledgments	Michael Collins, Assistant Director; Erin M. Godtland, Senior Economist, and Jennifer Gregory, Senior Analyst, led the engagement. In addition, James Bennett, Benjamin Bolitzer, David Chrisinger, Cynthia Grant, Jean Lee, Grant Mallie, Ashley McCall, Michael Morris, Rhiannon Patterson, Mark Ramage, James Rebbe, Douglas Sloane, Jeff Tessin, Shana Wallace, and Erin White made valuable contributions.

www.ingramcontent.com/pod-product-compliance
Lightning Source LLC
Chambersburg PA
CBHW081119290526
45795CB00006B/2171